Overworked and Underplayed?

30 Quick, Easy Ways to Boost Energy, Defuse Tension, and Make Fun of Life!

DR. MITZI L. GREGORY

Stress-Free Press

In recognition of the importance of preserving the written word,
The American Book Company has a policy to print books of value
in the United States on acid-free paper and we exert our
best commitment to that end.

Copyright © 2001 Dr. Mitzi L. Gregory

Published by Stress-Free Press

All Rights Reserved. No part of this book may be reproduced in whole
or in part in any form whatsoever without written permission
of the publisher or the author. Requests for permission
or further information should be addressed to

Stress-Free Press
4631 Four Seasons Terrace, Suite F
Glen Allen, VA 23060

Library of Congress Cataloging-in-Publication Data

Gregory, Mitzi L.-1955
Overworked and Underplayed?
No index
ISBN 1-928948-02-2
1. Stress Management. 2. Relaxation.
3. Building Energy and Enthusiasm. 4. Life Balance. 5. Peace of Mind.

Managing Editor: Don J. Beville

Editors: Susan Beach and June Sulc

Marketing Consultant: Kathy Hall

Text and Cover Design: Designer's Ink

Printed in the United States of America by
The American Book Company
7105 Winding Creek Lane, Lower Level
Chesterfield, VA 23832 (804-276-3201)

For information on ordering this title please contact our Web Site at:
www.drmitzi.com

10 9 8 7 6 5 4 3 2 1

Acknowledgements

Thanks and appreciation to all of my inspirers and supporters! To Maggie Bedrosian and Lynne Waymon for getting me started along the writer's path and for their words of wisdom regarding how to navigate the publishing maze. To Connie and Hank Diehl for listening to my nebulous ideas, and encouraging me to get past my fears and start writing! To Bart Grimes for loving and always believing in me, for making me laugh and teaching me to play on a daily basis, and for his nudges to stop polishing and start publishing.

For my greatest advocates and coaches, Susan Beach and June Sulc, I have a well of admiration. "Thank you" does not adequately express all I want to say to you! With their sharp eyes and nimble brains they poured over my manuscript *for countless hours* offering content and editing suggestions. This book would not have been possible without their support, encouragement, love, and patience.

I am thankful to Kathy Hall of *Marathon Marketing* for sharing the depth of her professional knowledge, for her great inventiveness and for her wonderful ability to tap my creative well. My gratitude also goes out to Kathy for introducing me to Don Bevillo of the *American Book Company*. Don's ability to stay calm and focused during times of challenge is amazing, and is only surpassed by his extensive knowledge of the publishing world. Thank you for pulling this all together, Don.

Saying that I am indebted to Linda Berry of *Designer's Ink* is an understatement. Linda is a layout/graphics wizard! I appreciate her outstanding listening skills, her intuitive insight and her creative elegance and grace. You have surpassed my expectations!

My gratitude goes out to my clients and seminar participants from whom I learn continually. Thanks also go to Lin and Mike Koch, Sally Hedleston, Billie Weadon, and Dawne Brooks Gulla for their suggestions and for being my playmates. I am forever indebted to my parents, Cora Lee and Art Gregory, for giving me a thirst for knowledge, the gift of gab, and for teaching me to love the written word.

And finally, thanks in advance to you, my readers, for sharing *your* ideas with me regarding energy enhancement, stress reduction, and making fun of life. Please send *your* suggestions to: 4631 Four Seasons Terrace, Suite F, Glen Allen, VA 23060. Looking forward to hearing from you!

Introduction

The little girl to the left of the page is me at age two and a half. My Dad had this picture laminated and carried it around in his wallet for years and years. Today I keep it in my daily planner to help me remember to schedule in time for joy, delight, and play.

When I look at that small face I see mischief, excitement, and energy - all of the qualities I work to include in my grown-up life. On the back of the picture I have the quote, "We don't quit playing because we grow old, we grow old because we quit playing." I am not sure who originally said that but for me he or she ranks right up there with Plato and Socrates. I *choose* to continue playing and creating a vibrant, energizing life.

My playful husband, Bart, has been teaching me to juggle. At first, I kept hitting myself in the head but I refused to give up. At one point in my life I was also hitting myself in the head in a figurative sense by over-scheduling commitments. I was the original all-work-and-no-play-girl, reluctant to say no, perfectionistic, and expending the majority of my energy and enthusiasm on work. I love being a career counselor, a coach, a professional speaker, and an author, yet I had let my work become all consuming. I drove myself to a point where I was overworked and underplayed, and decided it was time to stop hitting myself in the head and develop a set of more effective coping tools.

Overworked and Underplayed is the result of more than 18 years of intensive research and seminar leadership. I have utilized these life management tools in coaching thousands of individuals to create fulfilling lives, and have noted that a number of concepts for designing effective, balanced lives have been forgotten by these clients or, in some cases, seemed completely foreign to them.

First, for most of my clients the pace was merciless. They were hurtling through life, living at the speed of light. Time seemed to be compressed, and days passed by in a blur. Their high-pressured lives moved at such a frantic pace that they had gotten out of touch with who they were and with what was currently important to them. My clients were not only feeling disconnected from their *own* needs and desires, they were feeling disconnected from other people as well. They were so busy earning a living and/or raising a family that they were forgetting to *enjoy the process* of daily living.

They were also *waiting* until they had some free time to even think about relaxation and pleasure. As a result, *if* they ever found 5 or 10 spare minutes, they were either too tired to be creative and select something fun, new and stimulating *or* to enjoy the good things that life has to offer. My clients weren't noticing and appreciating the simple pleasures that surround us all, such as a glorious sunset, or the beautiful fire and richness of the changing fall foliage.

Secondly, many were permanently stuck in *serious mode* and had forgotten how to play. Fun was just one more thing there didn't seem to be enough hours in the day for. They couldn't tell me *any* hobbies that they enjoyed or *any* activities they engaged in purely for fun or pleasure. They were underplayed, suffering from *play anorexia*. All of their activities seemed to be goal or results-driven. Life was one long, non-stop to-do list. These clients were weary and exhausted. Between home and career demands, they were working themselves to death.

Finally, my clients (as well as many of my friends and colleagues) were universally stressed out, or in clinical terms *loosing their marbles*. They reported that there was no time to exercise or relax. Almost no time was spent with friends, and they did not spend the kind of *quality time* that they would prefer with their children, spouses, or significant others. The people who were *most* important were getting the *least* from them. They felt guilty and this guilt was causing them to feel even *more stressed out*.

Life was *not* intended to be an endurance test! If you have forgotten how to enjoy yourself, are yearning to play, are overly tense, exhausted, or out of touch with what brings you a sense of well-being, **Overworked and Underplayed** is for you! You were born for play, fun and wonder. It is time to reclaim the energy and exuberance of your childhood and bring balance, relaxation and joy back into your life. It's time to make fun of life!

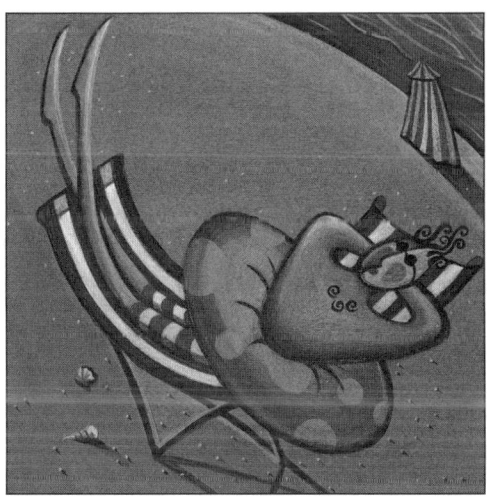

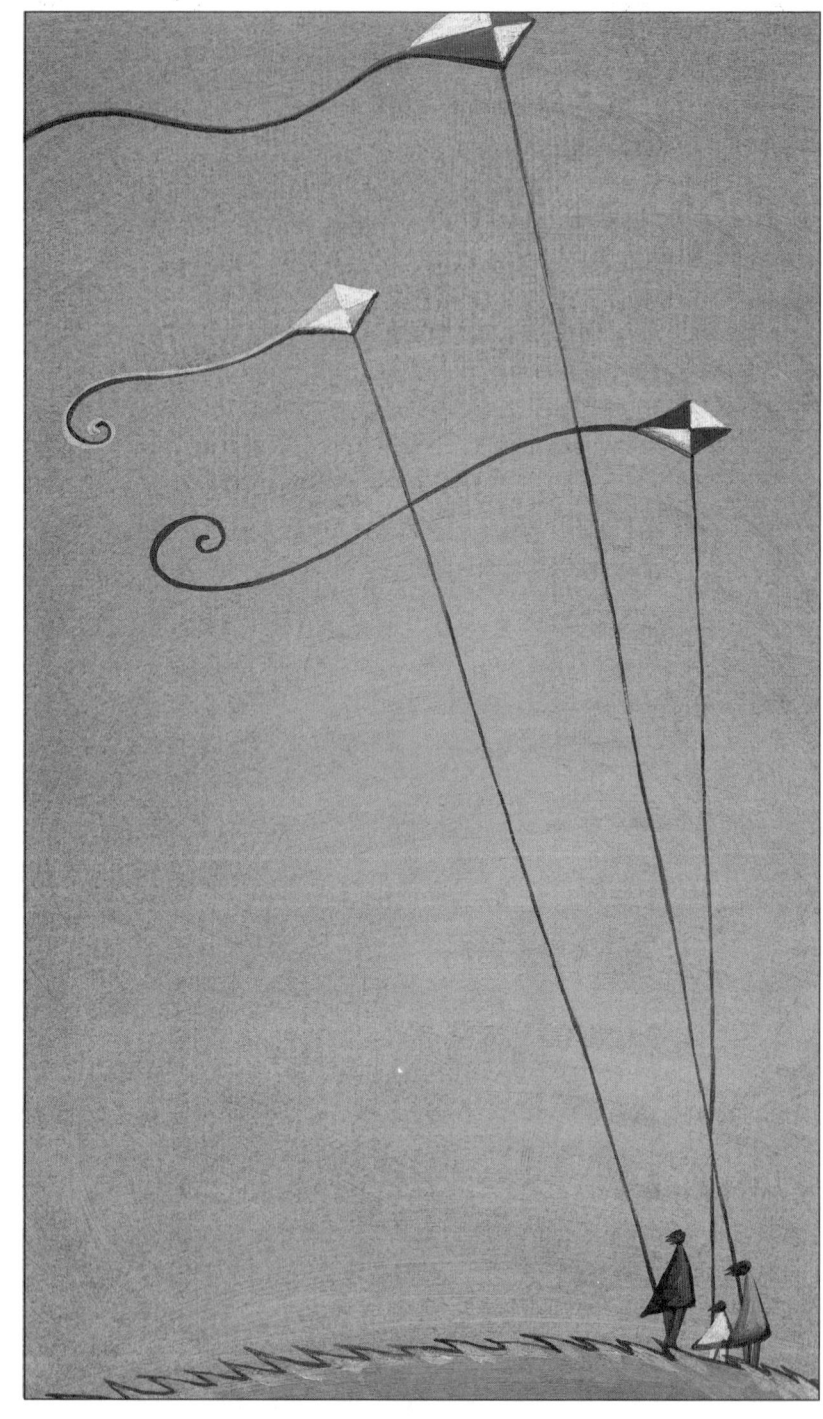

How to Use this Book

"Things do not change, we change."

-Henry David Thoreau

Overworked and Underplayed is all about YOU and meeting your unique needs. Use it as a personal mini-retreat to look inward, get in touch with your thoughts, feelings, needs, and priorities, and balance your career and your life.

Overworked and Underplayed will help you pinpoint *small* changes that you can make on a daily basis to boost your energy, reduce stress, and add more fun to your life. It is written in a light, humorous style to immediately enhance the quality of your life. Each chapter focuses upon simple, quick and easy techniques that you can readily incorporate into your non-stop, action-packed days.

Overworked and Underplayed was written with extremely busy, time-starved individuals in mind. All but the introductory chapter in each section can be read in five minutes or less.

Slough off old rules and constraints! You don't have to read **Overworked and Underplayed** from cover to cover, so have fun with it! Review the table of contents and pick out any chapter that appeals to you, one that meets your immediate needs.

x   How to Use this Book

If you are feeling burned out, like a wind up toy nearly at its end, see Part I, *More Energy, More Life!* which is filled with practical tools to renew your spirit and replenish your energy reserves. Burnout has been described as a failure to self-regulate, and *More Energy, More Life!* is packed with practical, doable self-care regulators to restore your personal fountain of energy.

How effectively do you manage stress and life balance? If you'd like to begin practicing safe stress, then Part II is for you. *Practice Safe Stress!* is full of tools to keep you calm when your life gets complicated. It will help you catch your breath, unfrazzle your jangled nerves, relax your body, calm your mind, cultivate a serene spirit, and start stress-proofing your life in small, measurable ways that really add up over time.

If you desire more fun in your life, Part III, *Make Fun of Life!* will provide you a temporary respite from adulthood, help you focus on doing *more* of the things you love and recapture the light-hearted exuberance of your youth. Experiment with the various methods in *Make Fun of Life!* for adding more joy, playfulness, and merriment to your days.

To improve the quality of your life you'll want to *take action*! Some people get stuck on "ready aim, aim, aim…" and *never* take action. Don't fall into that trap! Improving the quality of your life requires that new skills be practiced until they become a *habit*, a natural part of your daily routine. This doesn't mean you have to totally alter your *entire* life overnight. Consider changing a little at a time. Small steps are the keys to your success.

Habits are formed and changed over time. You will want to revisit certain chapters in **Overworked and Underplayed** in order to reinforce and master new, more effective behaviors. Also, periodically revisit **Overworked and Underplayed** as your needs change.

If you are overworked and underplayed, overly tired, hungry for balance, and ready to begin living more fully, turn to the contents and take that first step. Pick a chapter that sounds meaningful, and let's get started!

"Dr. Mitzi's book fills the prescription for those overworked, overwhelmed, and overdue for a personal overhaul! As a Certified Leisure Professional, I highly recommend her advice for playing as hard as we work to achieve a more balanced lifestyle."

-Gail Howerton, MA, CLP
Author of *Hit Any Key to Energize Your Life*

"Mitzi Gregory's new book is an upbeat and inspiring approach to re-energizing our lives... **Overworked and Underplayed** will not only motivate you to rediscover your sense of joy and fun, but will show you how to do so..."

-Susan Wilkes, Ph.D.
Organizational Psychologist
Manager, Workplace Initiatives
Virginia Commonwealth University

"Ahhh, this book is a welcome massage for my jumbled mind. It helps me relax again and be the person I sometimes forget to be as I speed through my grown-up life. Dr. Gregory blends warmth, wisdom and solid suggestions to remind me of the things my heart is whispering and my tired brain was shouting. This soothing and stimulating book rekindles my playful side. A great gift for a friend or for yourself."

-Maggie Bedrosian
Author of *Life is More Than Your To-Do List*

"Dr. Mitzi Gregory will have you dancing down the aisles of the grocery store! **Overworked and Underplayed** contains a multitude of ideas for de-stressing each day and recapturing the joyful spirit of childhood. An amazing number of strategies are presented for achieving balance—physically, mentally, and emotionally."

-Bonnie Miller
Career Counselor and Partner
The BrownMiller Group

Table of Contents

PART 1   More Energy, More Life!

1	Running on Empty?	3
2	"Happy Birthday to Me!"	13
3	Collecting Gold Stars	15
4	Memories of Scents Past	18
5	Got the "Too Cold to Go Out and Play" Blues?	20
6	Dream a Little Dream	22
7	The Power of Music	25
8	Luxuriate in the Sunshine	28
9	Creating Happily Ever After	30

PART 2   Practice Safe Stress!

10	Time to Play Hooky?	35
11	Run Away From Home	53
12	A Change of Pace	56
13	It's Naptime!	58
14	Tickle Your Fancy	61
15	Time Out	64

16	You Don't Have to Cook a Turkey	67
17	Are You the Manager of Your Universe?	70
18	"To Do" or "Not to Do"... That is the Question	72
19	A Talk with Your Imaginary Friend	74
20	Beat the Clock	76

PART 3 Make Fun of Life!

21	Recapture the Delight of Recess	81
22	Are We Having Fun Yet?	93
23	Create a Feast for Your Senses	96
24	All Work and No Play?	99
25	What's New?	101

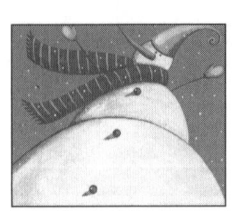

26	Who Do You Play With?	104
27	A Treasure Trove of Fun	107
28	Absent or Present?	110
29	Does a Puppeteer Pull Your Strings?	113
30	Go Dilly-Dally!	116
	Bibliography	119
	Practical Tools to Revitalize Your Life	121

More ENERGY
More LIFE!

PART 1

1. Running on Empty?

*"You have the capacity to balance yourself,
to set your own priorities."*

-Linda and Richard Eyre
Lifebalance

How can such a few words say so much? I have the capacity to create balance and to set my own priorities. Wow! I have *permission* to do that? When I discovered this concept in the Eyres' first edition of *Lifebalance*, it was a revelation. I was running as fast as I could, on the road at least 70% of my life, trying to provide outstanding services to my clients. I was a one-woman army trying to be an outstanding wife, mother, daughter, sister, niece, granddaughter, colleague, neighbor, employee, and friend. I was continually exhausted, running on empty, and totally out of balance.

That's when I realized that I was focusing all of my time, talents, and energy on the *needs of others*. I was living a self-denial lifestyle. A hard concept to grasp when you are in the midst of it. It's like the old saying, "A fish can't see the water he's in." My friend, Barbara, asked me one day, "Do you want to make a commitment to yourself or *be committed*?" She was joking, of course, but made a powerful point. That's when I recognized that there are *three* important facets to life balance, *not* just the two that I was focusing upon. There is *work* (paid or unpaid), there are *relationships*, and there is *self*.

The quest for balance is a universal struggle. When you are running a mile a minute, it is essential to make time for your *self*. It's a fact that individuals who continually work hard on their jobs and on giving to others, while ignoring their own needs, burnout. They have nothing left to give their families, friends, colleagues, and clients. Self-nourishment is essential for recharging and replenishing our energy reserves. We can't nourish others from a dry well. When we pay attention to and take care of our *own* needs we can give from our surplus, from our abundance.

Before you start to feel like you are running on empty, take time to re-energize. Give your *self* an energy transfusion anytime you are in need of unfrazzling. For an energy transfusion, seek out and engage in self-nurturing activities. Self-nurturing activities are pleasurable diversions, which provide a respite from life's daily challenges. They revitalize you; make you feel more energetic and vigorous.

Self-nurturing activities are small, concrete, loving actions that pamper your mind, body, and soul. Self-nurturing activities are performed solely for your own enjoyment, and leave you smiling, exuberant, and overflowing with the joy of living. They are uplifting life enhancers which restore your resilience. Any restorative activity that makes you *feel valued* and makes your heart sing qualifies.

Here are some examples of Self-nurturing activities:

- Participate in a hobby
- Visit a park, woods, or a forest
- Listen to your favorite music
- Enjoy a relaxing, warm bubble bath
- Plan a trip or vacation (or, if funds are tight, stop in a travel agency and pick up brochures for exotic destinations and daydream!)

Running On Empty?   5

- Tend to your garden and create beauty
- Go for a walk*
- Daydream*
- Stargaze*
- Have breakfast in bed
- Stop and enjoy the beauty of nature*
- Look through decorating magazines
- Relax in a whirlpool or sauna
- Go on a hot air balloon ride
- Visit a museum or art gallery
- Enjoy some time alone*
- Go on a house and/or garden tour
- Set up a girl's (or guy's) night out to spend time with your friends
- Browse through a toy store*
- Take a nap*
- Give a loved one a big hug*
- Do gentle stretching exercises*
- Reflect on your Gold Stars*
  (See Chapter 3 regarding developing a compliment list)
- Watch a sunrise or sunset*
- Relax in front of a warm fire*
- Read the daily comics for a laugh. Laughter triggers a biochemical response in the body similar to exercise, creating a healthy, positive state of mind.
- Visit a bookstore
- Receive a massage
- Engage in inspirational reading*
- Capture your thoughts and feelings in a journal*
- Put together a jigsaw puzzle
- Visit a magic shop and learn to do a magic trick

MORE ENERGY, MORE LIFE!

- Subscribe to uplifting magazines and/or newsletters
- Enjoy surrounding yourself with silence*
- Spend a few moments de-cluttering your surroundings*
- Read or listen to motivational books or audiotapes
- Go horseback riding
- Go to a silly movie that nobody else will go to see with you
- Have a gourmet cup of coffee or tea—cut out caffeine after noon to improve the quality of your sleep
- Engage in deep diaphragmatic breathing*
- Sing, hum, or whistle a happy tune*
- Play a musical instrument or begin music lessons
- Write a quick note, send a card or email to a cherished friend or relative
- Go to or rent a movie
- Engage in safe sex
- Rock in a rocking chair*
- Attend a sporting or athletic event
- Read your favorite book from childhood or any other type of *relaxing* book (nothing work related!)
- Meditate*
- Smile—this takes less energy than frowning because fewer muscles are engaged *and* you feel more optimistic*
- Reflect on your most enjoyable memories*
- Take time to get a haircut or try out a new hairstyle
- Go to church or synagogue*

> "An ounce of renewal is worth a pound of repair."
>
> -Maggi Bedrosian
>
> *Life Is More Than Your To-Do List*

- Visit your favorite jewelry store
- Go to a farm and pet the animals*
- Practice yoga*
- Relax in a hammock*
- Enjoy a cool, refreshing glass of water or fruit juice - add a slice of lemon or lime to make it more visually appealing
- Attend a workshop and learn something
- Go sailing or paddleboating
- Create something in clay or pottery
- Pet or frolic with an animal*
- Watch your favorite TV show*
- Attend a class reunion or reconnect with an old friend
- Collect a bouquet of wildflowers or buy yourself flowers
- Watch clouds and relax*
- Do some shoulder rolls to release tension*
- Enjoy a decadent dessert—in moderation, of course!
- Color, paint, or draw
- Go to a library*
- Attend a play or concert
- Engage in the exercise of your choice*
- Listen to a relaxation tape or do a relaxation exercise
- Participate in your favorite sport or game*
- Engage in T'ai Chi
- Work out with weights
- Organize your cherished photos in an album
- Sit in the sunshine*
- Visualize and concentrate on a relaxing scene*
- Go shopping or window-shopping

- Pray*
- Swim, float, wade, or relax in a pool or at the beach
- Go bowling
- Treat yourself to a nutritious meal at a restaurant you enjoy
- Visit a zoo
- Call a special friend or loved one*
- Go to a comedy club
- Dance*
- Have lunch or spend time with a supportive friend
- Reward yourself with a special gift that you can afford
- Go to a chiropractor for an adjustment
- Have a facial
- Ride a bike or motorcycle
- Massage fragrant lotion or oil into your tired feet or, better yet, have someone else do it!
- Browse through a craft store*
- Pack yourself a healthy lunch and enjoy it in a quiet spot *outside* of the office or your home
- Tell jokes and laugh*
- Learn a new skill or hobby
- Tell yourself the words you most want to hear from others*
- Visualize yourself achieving your goals*
- Schedule an annual check up for yourself
- Have a manicure and/or pedicure or give yourself one
- Call a cleaning service and have *them* clean your house or arrange to have someone else do your yard work
- Plan a spa get away or visit a day spa
- Take a multivitamin daily
- Research your family tree

Running On Empty? 9

- Read poetry*
- Play with your children or grandchildren*
- Learn a foreign language
- Explore an antique store*
- Go fishing
- Do something adventurous you've always wanted to try (for example, learn to hang glide)
- Focus on and appreciate your many blessings —write down at least five things you are grateful for every day*
- Bake bread
- Arrange flowers in a vase or bowl
- Write a poem
- Positively program your mind and increase your self-esteem by listening to affirmations - "How to be Your Own Fairy Godmother" by Dawne Brooks Gulla is an excellent choice. Call 1 (800) 409-9458 ext. 04 to order. You might also want to order your own magic wand.

(*= Free Activities)

> Self-nurturing activities are sources of personal pleasure, and are essential for boosting your spirit. They are life giving, vital nutrients which feed your body, comfort your spirit, and enrich your life.

Caution: *Self*-nurturing activities are want to's, *not* should's, or have to's. They involve investing quality time in your *self*, and may be done alone or with someone whom you *enjoy* spending time.

What would stoke the fire within you? What would bring you contentment and inner pleasure? There are limitless possibilities for refueling your tank, and giving your *self* an energizing transfusion. *Self*-nurturing activities are a balm for your soul. They make you glow from within, and restore your zest and zeal.

Engaging in at least one *self*-nurturing activity *each day* will provide you with a consistent sense of pleasure, and have a restorative effect. *Self*-nurturing activities make you feel like a million, and the cumulative effects of a few nurturing moments daily really add up over time.

I know what you are thinking. You are saying to yourself, "This woman doesn't understand how busy I am. She doesn't know how many hours I am putting in already. How can I possibly find 5, 10 or 15 *more* minutes for myself?" Julia Cameron in her inspiring, insightful book *The Artist's Way* sums up these feelings brilliantly, "Any bit of experimenting in self-nurturance is very frightening for most of us" (p.51). We get out of the *habit* of thinking about our own needs and taking care of ourselves. As a result, *self*-nurturing becomes foreign to us, and it's uncomfortable and frightening to get out of our comfort zones.

No Excuses—Try It!

Experiment. Invest a few minutes and you'll be hooked! These small investments in your *self* are life altering. You'll feel regenerated. Try out one of the *self*-nurturing activities on the list *or* create your own *self*-nurturing activity list. *You know* what makes you feel nourished, valued, and revitalized. *You know* what makes you sparkle. Which of those activities have you *not* engaged in for a while? What do you *enjoy* but haven't made time for recently? Honor your *self* and do it! It may take a lot *less* time than you think and will considerably increase your energy and enthusiasm levels. Show your *self* compassion. Enjoy your *self*. You owe your *self* a treat!

> " It is good for the soul to feed it what it wants, or it will always be hungry no matter what else you give it."
>
> - Gail Howerton
> *Hit Any Key to Energize*

Develop a sense of entitlement and learn to *be awake* to the needs of your *self*. Listen to your body, and your soul. Gail Howerton wisely points out that, "It is good for the soul to feed it what it wants, or it will always be hungry no matter what else you give it," (p. 46) in her book *Hit Any Key to Energize*.

Be respectful of your *self*. Practice kindness toward your *self*. Treat your *self* with compassion. Enjoy a brief *self*-nurturing diversion. Live it up and lavish your *self* with enjoyment. Value your *self*. Create champagne moments, and revel in pleasure. Enjoy *self*-renewal! *Self*-nurturing activities are life giving and they lift your spirits.

Remember that energy, satisfaction and enjoyment of life come from balancing *three* components - work, relationships, and self. It's a delicate balance, a balance worth integrating into each day. Focusing upon *self* and engaging in *self*-nurturing activities will create a dramatic and lasting change in your life. Engage in at least one *every day!* Wouldn't you like to experience a little pampering right now? No more running on empty, what will you do to nourish and sustain your *self* today?

2 · "Happy Birthday to Me!"

"The moments you celebrate become the years you cherish."

-Hallmark

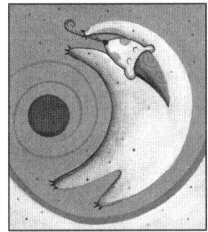

How do you mark the date of your arrival into the world? Your birthday is a time to celebrate and remember. Why not create a day of total peace and contentment?

This year I had a celebration *week*, instead of one day. It started out with a champagne brunch at one of my favorite restaurants. Since my birthday fell on Monday, my husband, Bart invited a number of our good friends to join us the Sunday before my birthday. We enjoyed a leisurely brunch and lively conversation before I opened my presents. My inner fun-ster still rejoices *any* time that I receive presents! I love the surprises those gaily wrapped treasures contain.

On my birthday, I like to honor my Mother in some way, whether it is sending her flowers to thank her for having me, or spending time with her, or both. Since I had taken the day *off* to honor myself (try it!), I invited my Mother out to lunch.

Mom has always been fascinated by anything British, so we went to *The English Garden* for lunch.

The English Garden is a quaint little combination gift shop and tearoom with eight small tables inside. After browsing through the exquisite imported gifts and gardening goodies we enjoyed an unhurried, quiet lunch served with tea, of course. It was very enjoyable to spend time focusing only on Mom; catching up on her life and thoughts. We even spent a few moments reminiscing about the day I was born.

After taking Mom home, I had a massage. Massages are a necessity for me, not a luxury. They help me relax, unwind, and bring me a sense of utter peace. I also find that I am more creative and better able to develop unique, new solutions to daily problems after a massage. Massages are self-nurturing activities, and one way that I honor myself on a regular basis. Following this celebratory ritual, I went home and took a nap.

Later that evening we went to my parents' house for drinks, hor d'oeurves, and cake. I love cake! What a delicious way to end a fun birthday.

I continued to feel special that week, when treated to lunch by various friends, and when celebrating with my stepchildren and their families. It's a pleasure to draw the celebration out! My friend Susan and I ate our dessert *first* during our celebration, and we felt like playful, naughty children. What fun!

Some days are meant to be remembered. How will you celebrate your birthday? How will you honor and nurture yourself? What little luxuries will you plan for your special day? Lavish yourself. Toast yourself. Do *not* wait for anyone else to do it for you. A birthday is a rare occasion, and you deserve a special, red-letter day. Honor your own needs and do *only* what you would like to do all day. Celebrate with a flourish!

3 • Collecting Gold Stars

"Dwell on compliments."

-Anita Gates

As a child, I was so proud to come home from piano lessons and show my family all the gold stars I had received. My talented, patient teacher, Mrs. Shelton, would give me gold stars whenever I mastered a piece that she had assigned. Sometimes I would have to practice and practice *for hours* to receive those treasured signs of recognition. I adored Mrs. Shelton (still do!) and enjoyed the sense of accomplishment associated with earning those gold stars.

As an adult I choose to focus upon a different type of gold star. Today I collect compliments instead. Compliments are a form of recognition for our talents, gifts and accomplishments. I find tuning-in to compliments to be energizing. Compliments can boost our self-esteem and confidence *if* we focus upon and accept them.

According to the National Association for Self-Esteem, two out of three Americans suffer from decreased self-esteem. They feel just good enough about themselves to *get by*, but don't live life as fully or as happily as they might, nor do they live up to their full potential.

Sanford and Donovan, authors of *Women and Self-Esteem: Understanding and Improving the Way We Think and Feel About Ourselves* note, "One common manifestation of low self-esteem is the inability to accept a compliment "(p.322). I am surprised by the number of grown-ups who slough off, dismiss, and ignore compliments. Why would anyone fall into such a trap? Why *choose* to reject an opportunity to feel good about yourself? Why not add up the *pluses*? Why not savor small successes?

> Compliments are a form of recognition for our talents, gifts and accomplishments. I find tuning-in to compliments to be energizing.

Compliments are a soothing antidote for the negative, cynical, self-critical mindsets and attitudes that are so pervasive today. Many are all too willing to focus on and accept criticism, yet they forget the importance of *balancing* their watchfulness by hearing and accepting praise and compliments, as well. Our mindset focus is something that we can readily change *if we practice*. Dwell on compliments. Rake them in!

Compliments are gifts that others give us, which express how they see us, and what they appreciate about us. Graciously accepted compliments can nourish your spirit and boost your self-esteem. You graciously accept a compliment any time you *merely* say, "Thank you." Period! Don't diminish the power of the gift you are receiving by saying anything to *deflect* the compliment, such as "It was an easy project. If I'd had more time I could have done a better job." Instead say, "thank you" and savor the moment.

Sanford and Donovan also suggest that you write down all of the compliments that you receive, then go back and read them on tough days when you may be feeling down or overwhelmed. These special words are a validation of your unique strengths and assets. Review your compliment list *often*, linger over the positive messages, and let them sink in. These frequent reviews will help you work toward self-acceptance and self-appreciation. Reviewing your compliment list often will also help you to feel good on a consistent basis. Compliments are motivation builders; they boost energy and enhance moods.

Embrace compliments. Record each one. Perhaps your inner fun-ster might like to add gold stars beside each entry. How many gold stars can YOU collect? Reach for the stars!

> Review your compliment list often, linger over the positive messages, and let them sink in.

4. Memories of Scents Past

"Smell is a potent wizard that transports us
across thousands of miles and
all the years we have lived."

-Helen Keller

The scent of fragrant honeysuckle wafting through the breeze brings to me the energizing sensation of running barefoot on a leisurely summer day. The enticing odor of bread baking conjures up divine memories of sitting in Granny's kitchen anxiously awaiting the delicious rolls she was so gifted at making. My brother and I raced to get out the butter and apple butter as soon as we could smell those tantalizing treasures. Then we sat in Granny's kitchen savoring the anticipation.

Each of us has our own unique storehouse of scent-linked memories; rich with special times and people. Why is it that scents have such a strong, clear connection to poignant memories? It is because our olfactory sense is linked directly to the most primitive area of the brain, the limbic region, where memory, sexuality, creativity, as well as moods and emotions, operate. Certain aromas not only impact us psychologically, but also on a physiological level by promoting deep, slow breathing and general relaxation, or by enhancing concentration and productivity.

In fact, one of the gifts brought to Christ was frankincense, which aromatherapists recommend as an anti-inflammatory, a sedative, a diuretic, and to aid digestion, among other things. For more on the curative effects of scents see Julia Lawless's *The Complete Illustrated Guide to Aromatherapy: A Practical Approach to the Use of Essential Oils for Health and Well-being.*

Cleopatra's devotion to scents is legendary. She used pleasurable smells to enhance basic, sensual enjoyment. Prior to receiving Marc Antony, Cleopatra had the sails on her cedarwood ships perfumed, had incense burners arranged to ring her throne, and was anointed from head to toe with fragrances. It is also said that she entertained him on a bed of rose petals.

> During thousands of years of experimentation aromatherapists have used scents for pleasure and as beauty treatments, as well as for health purposes such as to enhance moods and relieve stress. The ancient Chinese acknowledged that, "Every perfume is a medicine."

What scents delight you? To build energy and increase your productivity you might try the invigorating scent of citrus fruits such as lemons. Researchers in Japanese auto plants circulated essential oils of lemon through the air conditioning system and found that productivity increased 20-30%. Lemon oils diluted with purified water make a delightful mist that you can spray in your home and/or office. This cleansing mist is a great way to reclaim your space after stressful or unpleasant meetings or visits, or perhaps you might enjoy lighting a lemon-scented candle to achieve the same effect.

Rosemary is another pick-me-up, which stimulates the mind. Experiment to determine which aromas boost your energy levels. What scent memories might you tap into to boost your energy today? What enlivens you? Want to join me in kicking off my shoes, picking some honeysuckle, and running through the dew-covered grass?

5. Got the "Too Cold to Go Out and Play" Blues?

"How do you make your spirit smile?"

-Maggie Bedrosian
Life is More Than Your To-Do List

It has rained 22 of the 38 days we've had so far this year. No snow just repeated violent downpours with high winds. I am beginning to forget what the sun looked like! I've got the too cold to go out and play winter blues.

> Flowers make my spirit smile. Their fragile beauty makes me feel nurtured and appreciated. Flowers are chocolate for the eyes!

How can I lift my spirits and recapture my enthusiasm? Little glimpses of spring would do it. I am ready for springtime NOW! Maggie Bedrosian in her wonderful book *Life is More Than Your To-Do List* suggests that NOW stands for "Noticing, Ordinary, Wonders" (p. 63). Flowers are a springtime wonder.

I share the Victorian passion for flowers. Their grace and beauty touch my soul. Flowers are natural wonders, exotic treasures to perk up any day. Any time I want to be energized, I imagine a field of daffodils lazily nodding their heads in the gentle breeze of a spring day.

Over time, I have collected a number of small vases, and have enjoyed placing little bunches of *wonders* in the bathroom, on the breakfast table, on the mantel, on the dining room table, in the bedroom, on my desk, etc. One inexpensive bunch of fresh daisies will go a long way! Fresh flowers add joy to a room. Place them anywhere you will see them often to perk up a drab winter's day.

These little glimpses of springtime serve as a soothing, peaceful, pristine oasis for the winter weary, and as Thoreau said, "We can never have enough of nature." What *ordinary wonders* inspire you and perk you up? What reminds you of a lovely, cheerful spring day? How can you surround yourself with these wonders to energize yourself? Well, get moving! Not only will *you* feel more energized and joyful but so will all those who share your environment. Go make your spirit smile!

6 • Dream a Little Dream

"You've got to have a dream. If you don't have a dream, how you gonna have a dream come true?"

-Rodgers and Hammerstein
"Happy Talk"- South Pacific

Dreams fuel lives. *South Pacific's* Bloody Mary was motivated by her dream that her lovely daughter, Liat, marry well. Navy nurse, Nellie Forbush's dream was to lead an exciting, adventurous life. Nellie wanted to see what life was like outside of Little Rock, Arkansas. She also wanted to meet different kinds of people, and see if she liked them. Dreams are unfulfilled longings, and as Nellie implies as she sings the *"Cockeyed Optimist"*, I choose to believe that anything is possible.

> "The tragedy of life is what dies in the hearts of men while they live."
>
> -Albert Einstein

I admire those who take action to make their dreams come true. John Glenn's return to space rekindled my youthful fascination with the space program. What rational person would have dreamed that a 77 year-old American would be selected to engage in scientific research in outer space? Glenn reminded me of my own childhood visions of travelling through space, and I reveled in those warm, cherished memories. Remember your childhood dreams?

My friend, Lin, recently made one her husband's dreams come true for his birthday. Mike had always wanted a red sports car, yet with one child in college and another soon to be there that dream had been put on hold for a while. Lin is a gifted creative thinker with a huge, generous, loving heart. She rented Mike a red convertible for the weekend that his birthday fell upon. Mike celebrated that birthday in grand style! He came over to our house and beamed as he showed us *his* new car. That birthday will be remembered for a lifetime because he had a dream come true.

Albert Einstein said, "The tragedy of life is what dies in the hearts of men while they live." This statement is very profound and, unfortunately, too often true of *both* men and women. I am determined that as I look back over my life upon my ninetieth birthday that I will have led a rich, full life. I will not have regrets regarding unfulfilled dreams. I will not have *unlived* reveries.

The belief that dreams come true makes life more interesting, boosts our energy and provides an endless stream of long-lasting joy. What's your fondest dream? Some dreams are magical, yet they don't have to be the grand dream of a lifetime, or anything as exalted as space travel or ending world hunger. Your dream could be to begin music lessons, to learn to ride a horse, or to visit and explore a new city. What have you always wanted to try, learn, or experience? Spend a few minutes fantasizing. What unfulfilled longings did you uncover? Jot them down and continue to add to this list. This is Step 1 in "Dream Fulfillment 101".

How will you make these reveries a reality? If you are stuck, ask a friend to help you brainstorm ways to make one of your dreams come true. There is a big difference between dreaming and *doing*, so Step 2 is to *take action* to make your dream come true.

A dream is a wish your heart makes, so your dreams are just a heartbeat away. Listen to your heart's desire and turn it into a reality. Foster your dreams. Robert Browning said, "The best is yet to be…" and I believe he was right. Don't you? Don't delay your dreams. It's time to turn the things that you *want* to do into the things that you've *done*. Go make your dreams come true!

7 · The Power of Music

"Sounds have power."

-Wayne Dyer
The Secrets to Manifesting Your Destiny

Since the time of the ancient Greek philosopher and mathematician, Pythagoras, it has been noted that music creates a variety of physical and emotional responses. It can be utilized to change our moods and can evoke healing, relaxation or invigoration.

Invigoration is what the music did to us in San Juan. Puerto Ricans are festive night people. They are friendly, animated, and full of life! The people of San Juan love to get dressed up, dance, socialize, and be together. What fine

> Music fills our ears and then touches our souls.

musicians and dancers! They seem born to *merengue* and *salsa* and are happy to share their stirring, sensual dances with visitors.

The big hotel where we stayed had an ample dance floor and live music which seemed to pack in the *Sanjuaneros* at all hours of the day and night. Romantic trios opened the afternoons and evenings, followed by more lively rhythms inspired by this exuberant, exotic island.

Fun is what counts in Puerto Rico, so of course Bart and I were moved to try our own versions of *merengue* and *salsa*. What jubilant dances! It was easy to be swept away by such spirited music. It helped us connect with our jovial, lighthearted, playful sides. The music made us feel buoyant. I could have danced all night!

Mothers have known the power of music for eons, using lullabies to touch a soothing inner chord with weary, grouchy youngsters. Music can transform youngsters' moods and lull them off to peaceful sleep.

Want to increase your productivity? Music can help! According to Peter McLaughlin in *Catchfire*, "Baroque music such as Bach, Vivaldi, or certain kinds of upbeat jazz entrains your brain waves to high alpha frequency, which is associated with mental alertness and creativity" (p. 225). Experiment! What types of music do you enjoy? Might playing music help you work more productively?

Because we connect with music at an emotional level, it can be also be used to lift us from depression and to boost our confidence as was noted during a recent episode of *Ally McBeal*. The ever neurotic Ally visited her therapist (played by wacky Tracy Ullman) who suggested that Ally select a theme song to boost her sense of competence and power during troubled times. After experimenting with a number of tunes she selected a robust, convincing song to boost her confidence and even visualized back-up singers to support her, since there is strength in numbers.

What would your theme song be? What stirs you to action? What gives you confidence and a sense of power? What tunes sooth and relax you? Pay attention to the music that engulfs you. Is it supporting your current efforts or draining the life out of you? As Louis Armstrong said so eloquently, "What we play is life." Melodies have tremendous power over our moods, our energy and our productivity. What inner rhythms do you want to touch, tap in to, or promote? What harmonies will you use to sculpt your life? You've got the power. Who could ask for anything more?

8. Luxuriate in the Sunshine

"Keep your face to the sunshine and you cannot see a shadow."

-Helen Keller

Whenever we begin to plan a vacation I immediately envision the rich warmth of the sunshine gently caressing my body. For me the sun signifies relaxation and revitalization. The sun seems to be nature's nurturing hand soothing and melting tension from weary bodies, and boosting the spirit.

Even as a child I remember my thirst for the sun. It contributed to my fun, adding to my energy and enthusiasm. It graced our softball games, picnics, and neighborhood parades. I still enjoy closing my eyes, turning my face to the sun and letting its healing light soak into my pores. Those fond moments are then stored away to be recalled on cloudy, gray days.

Prevention magazine reported that "sunshine brings an unexpected health benefit" (March 1998, p.27). The article summarized research into health data for approximately 5,000 women and found that the risk of breast cancer was 30-40%

lower in the women who were getting the most sun. A corresponding decline was discovered in women who lived in sunny climates. The article goes on to report that vitamin D which is produced in our skin when exposed to sunlight may be the key to lowering breast cancer risks, and that 10 to 15 minutes of sun exposure a day *without* sunscreen will give your body the vitamin D it needs.

Of course we have all heard that *prolonged* exposure to the sun without sunscreen can raise the risk of skin cancer. Moderation appears to be the key in this case.

Exposure to the sun also makes you more alert because it suppresses melatonin, a hormone that causes an increased drive to sleep, according to Dr. Michael Thorpy, Director of the Sleep - Wake Disorders Center at Monteforte Medical Center in New York. Might a short stroll in the sunshine be beneficial to your health, renew your energy and enthusiasm, and perk up your mood? If you can't get outside move to a sunny room.

John Muir wrote, "The sun shines not on us, but in us". Why not absorb a bit of the sun's warmth and show the world *your* sunny side? It will make you feel sun-sational! Go find *your* place in the sun.

9. Creating Happily Ever After

"Romance is about the little things. It's much more about the small gestures - the little ways of making daily life with your lover a bit more special - than it is about extravagant, expensive gestures."

-Gregory J. P. Godek
1001 Ways to be Romantic

I grew up hearing romantic fairy tales in which the hero and the heroine would ride off into the sunset to live happily ever after; yet I've discovered that real life doesn't work quite the same way. Our complicated schedules, work and family demands, and the cumulative stressors that we each encounter daily make it a challenge to find time for romance.

By romance I mean time to enjoy your partner and to grow your love. It's focusing on little gestures that strengthen your union. Romance is as simple as an invitation to come and sit beside you. It's holding hands. It's taking a few minutes to dance with each other, even though you aren't Fred Astaire and Ginger Rogers. Even if you feel more like Fred and Wilma Flintstone, give it a try!

Romance is the means by which you make deposits into your emotional bank account as a couple. You make such deposits any time you give your partner your *undivided* attention. Remember when you would hang on your partner's every word? Making time for short periods of *focus* on your partner is essential for growing your love and making it timeless. Let the answering machine take your calls, focus on your partner, and act like you are dating all over again.

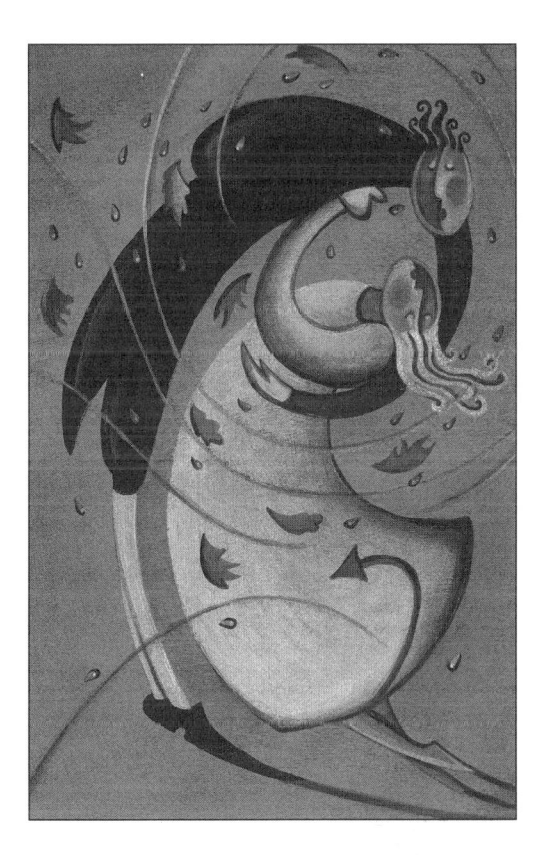

Life is not naturally romantic. Relationships have ebbs and flows when candlelight and love songs are replaced by changing diapers and attending little league games. Yet, you don't have to slide into the habit of taking your partner for granted! Do something unexpected or unpredictable. You can let your partner know that you think of him or her often with a quick note or card left where it is certain to be found (sealed with a kiss, of course). Or leave a brief message in his voice mailbox to greet him when he arrives at work. Bart made my day once by calling and singing a couple of lines of *"Some Enchanted Evening"* into my voice mailbox. I saved that message and replayed it any time I needed to be reminded that I am cherished, valued and loved.

Romance is in the details, and involves breaking out of ho-hum routines. Simple, little things evoke romance. We've started leaving a small, crystal votive candle on our table to remind us to create happily ever after moments at dinnertime. What was the first song the two of you ever slow danced to? Why not have that playing softly to kick off a few romantic minutes?

Think back. Remember when you fell in love? Where did you go? What did you do? If you saw a movie on your first date, perhaps you could rent it and take a trip down memory lane.

How might you make a deposit into your emotional bank account as a couple? How could you rekindle your passion? How can you strengthen your union and celebrate your love? Taking a walk and gazing at the stars? Exchanging a back rub? Reminiscing about the best meal you've ever had? The best night out on the town? Or future dreams? Perhaps you'd like to paint the town red or to create your own private Eden at home. Whatever you choose, the goal is to overwhelm yourselves with pleasure!

> Romance is in the details, and involves breaking out of ho-hum routines. Simple, little things evoke romance.

What would make you feel closer to your partner? Could you take turns planning romantic interludes? There are no rules as long as you fold expressions of love into each day. Let your imagination run wild. How can you make your partner feel more loved than ever? How will you create happily ever after today? Why not create a night laced with romance that you will always remember?

Note: Call 1 (800) 305-8888 for a catalogue from "The Romance Boutique". This catalogue is filled with games, clothing, jewelry, candles, etc. to help you celebrate your love.

Practice SAFE Stress!

PART 2

10. Time to Play Hooky?

"Work at play, play at work."

-Anonymous

Think of all of the breaks we had during our days when we were children. We had fruit break, potty breaks, lunch, naptime, recess, not to mention stretch breaks when we sang "Head, shoulders, knees, and toes" . . . while bending and pointing to the body part we were singing about at the time. No wonder children have so much energy! They instinctively pay attention to their minds and bodies, and take *frequent* breaks to recharge themselves and to help them better focus.

Our bodies and brains function best when we engage in an intense activity followed by a brief period of rest and recovery. How many breaks do you take a day? Do you even leave your desk during lunchtime? Do you take time to look out of your window, if you have one? If you start your day at 8 *sharp* and end the day at 5 *dull*, it's time to start playing hooky! Short breaks, lasting from one to ten minutes, scattered throughout the day serve as *recovery periods* which help you to clear your head, de-stress, refocus, re-energize, and develop more creative solutions to life's challenges.

Prominent mood, tension and energy researcher Dr. Robert Thayer found a direct correlation between tension and energy that is important to understand when considering breaks as methods for improving productivity and performance. In *The Origin of Everyday Moods: Managing Energy, Tension, and Stress* Thayer explains that constantly increasing tension reduces energy, while increasing energy decreases tension. He also reports that, "This is an important principle to recognize because it offers a practical way to counteract anxiety, tension, and nervousness: Engage in activities that raise energy" (p.68).

> **Listen to your body.**

How can you utilize this information? First, *you know* when you need a break. *Listen to your body.* Assess your current energy state and tension level, and then select the type of break that will benefit you at that particular moment. There are two types of breaks to capitalize upon. Breaks can be *either* little shots of adrenaline to get you charged up and energized *or* regenerative mini-vacations, pauses that calm and refresh you after dealing with a series of daily stressors.

Stress hormones produce a heightened state of mental and physiological arousal, and over time continual stress can wear your system down leading to exhaustion, depletion of your immune system, and a variety of potential physical ailments. If you are tense and filled with pent up stress, select a tension-taming break which will help your mind and body return to a relaxed state by releasing that excess tightness and anxiety in a positive manner. Movement is a good choice during tense times, or do some deep breathing, write in your journal to get your worries and frustrations on paper and release your pent up emotions, de-clutter your desk, play with a toy from your toy chest, or call a friend for a quick chat.

When your energy level is low and you feel brain dead, select an energy-boosting break. Our minds and bodies crave breaks as energy enhancers, disrupting the energy depletion cycle. Select energy boosters such as going for a walk to get your blood pumping, finishing some short task and enjoying the feeling of accomplishment, or listening to some energizing music. If you feel like your blood sugar level is low, eat a healthy snack such as ½ of a bagel (*sans* cream cheese), low-fat popcorn, low-salt pretzels, or better yet, fruit. The simple sugars found in fruits are the most easily accessible source of energy in terms of the digestive system, and the best source of short-term energy. Stay away from snacks loaded with refined sugar. *Healthy* snacks during your energy lulls will help you maintain a steady, constant energy level.

> Productivity, enthusiasm, and vigor are grounded in play, not work.

CAUTION: *According to stress researchers, everything that you eat has a biochemical effect upon your body impacting moods, behavior, energy level, the ability to think clearly, and to make good decisions. This is because food changes your blood sugar levels. Do not eat merely to comfort yourself when your stress levels are high. Comfort eating of high fat, sugary foods is a trap too many people fall into, which creates a quick surge of energy followed by a* drastic *energy decline, as well as feelings of mental sluggishness, physical fatigue, and the inability to perform at optimal levels.*

An hour after consuming high fat, sugary snacks your energy plummets to an *even lower level* than it was *before eating* the snack. By choosing healthy snacks you promote physical health and *constant* energy, not energy peaks and valleys that wear down the body.

When you feel stressed or your energy and ability to concentrate lag *listen to your body*! Go play hooky, and take a break. Try some of the following escapes to decrease your stress levels, increase your ability to concentrate, improve the quality of your thinking, expand your creativity, enhance your performance and productivity, be happier and healthier, and to boost your energy level.

To Enhance Concentration and Performance:

1. **STOP** eating lunch at your desk! Take your lunch outside and eat in a park, by a lake or at a picnic table. Or have lunch at a *new* restaurant instead of at your usual haunt.

2. **ENGAGE** in 10 deep abdominal breaths to get more oxygen into your system. Go against social conditioning and let your stomach expand to take in more energizing oxygen. Increased oxygen in the bloodstream and the brain leads to thinking clarity.

3. **ADD** affirmations to your deep breathing. For example, "I am" (as you breathe in) "relaxed" (as you breathe out) or "at peace" or "in control" or "centered" or "focused" or "energized". There are two rules to remember when developing effective affirmations. First, affirmations always need to be *positively* stated phrases. The unconscious mind filters out the "not" in "I am not tense," so it hears "I am tense" instead. Secondly, affirmations are short visualizations which need to be stated in the *present* tense. They are not about tomorrow or some time in the future, but *right now*. "I am relaxed", is your body's cue to respond to match what your mind is thinking. What the mind dwells on, the body acts upon. Affirmations are *mind massages*. They are self-talk in its highest form. Use affirmations to unclog your life of negativity and to enhance your concentration and performance.

4. **FOCUS** on the *progress* you have made during the last hour, and give yourself a pat on the back.

5. **USE** positive, supportive self-talk. Talk to yourself the same way you would speak to someone you cherish. This will significantly improve your performance and enhance your productivity.

6. I saw a bumper sticker the other day that said, "Kids need praise every day". So do adults! **SHOW** appreciation often. **PAY** someone a compliment. Give team members certificates of ward for outstanding performance or meeting tight deadlines, or give them a quick round of applause. You might also want to give them "I'm Appreciated" buttons. To order call (804) 273-0304.

> Affirmations are mind massages. They are self-talk in its highest form.

7. **PAY** *yourself* a compliment. It will boost your motivation.

8. **FINISH** something...anything! After tying up the loose ends, savor the sense of completion.

9. **WRITE** a compliment on a post-it-note and leave it for someone to find unexpectedly. Do this at home and at work.

10. **LOOK** through a book of quotes to find something new that inspires you.

11. **STOP** by a friend's desk and visit for a couple of minutes. Set the stage for a *positive, up beat, performance enhancing* conversation by asking the right questions. For example, ask them what their *greatest accomplishment* has been today or what has been the *best thing* that's happened to them. Use this technique during staff meetings also to boost employee motivation and morale.

12. **CELEBRATE** your successes! Reward yourself (and members of your team) for accomplishments. Gather your team together, say a few words, and clink your coffee mugs together in a celebratory toast. Or order pizza or have some ice cream together. For a simple celebration that lasts all day, bring in a balloon or two that team members pass around from desk to desk. That way everyone gets to have the "party" at his or her desk for an hour or two. Go to a dollar store and buy yourself and/or your team members a toy. Surprise your team with Tootsie Pops®. Different things motivate different people, so find out what might work for your team and vary the rewards each time. Little celebrations spur team members on to further accomplishments!

13. PROP your feet up for a few minutes. Or keep a stool under your desk to prop your feet up on. This is especially comfort enhancing for short people, like me. Greater comfort leads to greater productivity!

14. CLOSE your eyes, breathe deeply, and count backward from 100 slowly. This helps you relax and will improve your ability to concentrate.

15. LIGHT a candle in a scent that will increase your productivity and concentration. Research studies indicate that lemon is a good choice. Experiment to see what works best for you.

16. When you are racing the clock to meet a tight deadline and you find the gears of your mind jamming, SHIFT your activity to something *totally different* from what you have been doing for a few moments. Children understand the power of activity shifting, and readily change to another activity when they begin to loose their ability to focus on what they are currently doing. Grown-ups need to be reminded that activity shifting gives us a change in mental pace and provides a measure of restoration while still continuing working.

To Decrease Stress:

1. LISTEN to a stress management tape or CD. *"Stress-Free in 15 Minutes"* is an excellent escape from daily stressors. This relaxing audiotape/CD helps you release muscular tension, slow down your frazzled, overworked mind, and sleep more soundly. *"Stress-Free is 15 Minutes"* is an effective, restorative break while at work *or* at home! It also makes a great gift. To order call (804) 273-0304.

2. CLOSE your eyes to shut off outside stimulation for a couple of minutes. (Tip: Do NOT try this while driving!)

3. STAND UP and STRETCH, or bend forward as far as you can *comfortably* to stretch all of the muscles down your neck, back, and legs. Don't rush! Hold these stretches for 30 seconds to loosen muscles and retrain your body to relax.

4. DO some neck rolls. **Caution:** Do *not* roll your

Time to Play Hooky? 41

head *backwards!* Roll it to one side, down in the front, and to the other side advises my chiropractor, Dr. Ed Ashworth.

5. GIVE your neck and shoulders a mini-massage.

6. OPEN a window and enjoy some fresh air. Breathe deeply, and soak in your surroundings. Delight in the sounds of nature - the birds calling, the gentle patter of the rain, the crickets chirping, or a breeze blowing the leaves. This brief pause will renew your spirit and reduce your stress level.

7. TAKE a short mental vacation. Look at a postcard, travel brochure, or picture in a magazine depicting an inviting location. Visualize the tranquil, quiet woods or some other appealing environment. Studies conducted at Texas A&M University at College Station indicate that viewing soothing images of natural settings including greenery and/or water reduce blood pressure and muscle tension within five minutes. Remember: pleasant, peaceful images are physically relaxing, and help you replenish your energy reserves.

8. EMAIL or PHONE a friend or loved one for a quick hello. Shrug your shoulders or flex your feet while you are at it.

9. ENGAGE in some shoulder rolls.

10. GAZE at pictures of your loved ones or a picture from a fun or special occasion for a brief, pleasurable escape.

11. ENJOY an *unhurried* cup of coffee or tea, preferably decaffeinated.

12. WATER your plants and prune the dead leaves. This will give your plants a fresher look, and provide you with a relaxing escape. Activity shifting is a great way to decrease stress. Working with my plants is a *kinesthetic* activity, which gives my *mind* a short, relaxing break from its normal routine, and soothes my soul. It is also a satisfying break for me because I can see immediate, tangible results from my efforts.

13. SQUEEZE a stress ball or throw it up against the wall to release tension.

14. LOCK yourself in the bathroom for a few tranquil moments. Give yourself a few precious moments away from everyone else! No telephone! No interruptions! Enjoy the healing silence.

15. PASS part of a big project on to someone else. (This is my husband Bart's favorite—at work AND at home!)

16. HAVE conversation with a good listener.

17. Clutter is stressful, and we do not work at optimal levels surrounded by disorganization and clutter! SPEND five minutes de-cluttering your desk and/or your environment. If you find de-cluttering oppressive, call in an expert to do it for you. For more help with de-cluttering and becoming organized check out the Queen of Clutter's calendar, *"Organized at Last! A Tip a Day to Keep Clutter at Bay®"*. Contact the Queen, Pat Moore, at www.queenofclutter.com.

18. KEEP flowers on your desk. Take a few moments to slow down, and enjoy their beauty and their fragrance.

19. HAVE some Silly String® in your desk drawer to use as a stress release rather than saying something you'll later regret. A few squirts and you'll be laughing, instead of fuming.

20. Water pistol duels at "high noon" in a conference room are a great way to LET OFF steam.

21. To RELIEVE shoulder tension, do "push ups" in your doorway. Stand in the center of a doorway, and take one step back. Place your hands at shoulder height on either side of the outside of a doorframe, with your arms straight. Slowly bend your elbows and ease your body toward the doorway. Next, push yourself back out until your arms are straight again. Repeat. This is a great way to stretch out tight, tired shoulders and release pent up tension.

22. HAVE binoculars and a bird watching book ready for a short, relaxing escape.

23. USE a soothing screen saver such as a favorite nature scene or fish swimming for a serenity break.

24. DECORATE your office with peaceful art and take a few moments to enjoy its calming beauty for a relaxing interlude.

To Increase Energy and Beat the Afternoon Blahs:

1. TAKE a walk to the copy machine, mailroom, etc. Move around for a couple of minutes.

2. LAUGH! Look through a joke book, look up jokes on the Internet, or recall a humorous event. It's physically easier to smile than to frown. Smiling requires the use of fewer muscles so why not save some energy? Plus, smiles are wondrous things. Give them away and they multiple! Try it and see.

> **Note:** If you've been so busy that you have forgotten how to smile, try sleeping with a coat hanger in your mouth. This proven technique will put a perpetual smile on your face, according to comedian and professional speaker, Allie Bowling.

3. BEGIN a cartoon bulletin board and invite others to add their favorite cartoons.

4. ENJOY a satisfying, healthy treat.

5. SPLASH cool water on your face for an invigorating break.

6. MAKE plans for fun, something you'll look forward to. Enjoy the anticipation.

Time to Play Hooky?   45

7. MAKE your environment uplifting. Fill it with pictures of loved ones, exotic, restful vacation spots, and quotes that are motivating or that inspire you. Change these items periodically so that they will remain fresh and not become "invisible" to you.

8. OPEN your blinds and let in as much natural light as possible.

9. SEND a get well, birthday, anniversary, or thinking of you card to someone.

10. GO outside for a brief walk to clear your head, but remember to come back!

11. Go **GET** a glass of water. Do this *at least* eight times a day. Water helps your body with digestion and nutrient absorption. According to "Choices for Living Happier and Healthier" magazine, one symptom of dehydration is fatigue.

12. SEND a cheerful note or post card to someone special.

13. LAY DOWN on a sofa or the floor for a quick rest. You could hide under your desk like George did on *Seinfeld* so nobody would catch on!

14. VISIT a gift or consignment shop during lunchtime.

15. PLAY a computer game.

16. TAKE a power nap.

17. LOG ON to the Internet and visit a favorite site.

18. WATCH TV or a movie "short" during your lunch break.

19. EXERCISE during lunch. Physical activity increases blood sugar levels and circulation, revs up metabolism, and releases adrenaline which boosts your energy level.

20. Close your door, **TURN ON** a favorite song and have your own dance party.

21. To boost your energy level, HAVE a picture of a new car, sofa, beach house, etc. that you are working toward and look at it for a few minutes to remind you of your goal. Having *specific, measurable* goals that you can *clearly* visualize boosts motivation. What are you dreaming of? Use it as an energy boosting motivator!

22. GIVE each team member a kazoo and break out into song to increase your energy and encourage a playful team spirit.

23. USE brightly colored beach towels in your bathroom all year round.

24. SURROUND yourself with colors your love. Find file folders, paper clips, pens and pencils, etc. in your favorite colors to boost your energy.

To Enhance Creativity and Fun:

1. JUMP up and down a few times. (**Tip:** Take the change out of your pockets first, as it may be stressful to pick it up later.)

2. PLAY a harmless joke on someone.

3. SET UP a tennis match, a golf game, or some other fun sporting event.

4. SPEND a minute or two daydreaming. (**Tip:** Keep a pencil in your hand so your boss won't notice!)

5. LOOK through your favorite magazine or read a brief article. This brief respite will clear and renew your mind.

6. RUN or WALK UP and down the stairs instead of taking the elevator. It will enliven you, and burn off a few calories.

7. TELL your favorite joke or story.

8. DOODLE or color in a coloring book.

9. WHISTLE or SING your favorite tune.

10. FOLD a paper airplane and sail it across your office.

11. MAKE faces. This is a good way to relax your facial muscles. It will also make you laugh if you do it in front of a mirror.

12. LEAVE a silly, clever or humorous message on someone's answering machine. Disguise your voice if you are really feeling playful.

13. PLAY with your favorite toy.

14. KEEP in mind the words of Cicero while focusing on creativity enhancement, "Only the person who is relaxed can create, and to that mind ideas flow like lightning." Close your door or go to a conference room and relax by meditating for a few minutes.

15. GO to lunch with a friend or coworker with a well-developed sense of humor or playfulness.

16. GAZE out of your office window. Enjoy the beauty of nature and your environment.

17. PLAY your favorite music. Music unlocks your creativity and imagination by activating the right hemisphere of your brain.

18. SPIN playfully around and around in your desk chair.

19. CHANGE you office around. Focus on creating greater comfort. What layout would keep you out of drafts from heating and cooling systems? How could you keep the glare off of your computer screen? What arrangement would keep you from being continually interrupted? Be imaginative! This change will give you a fresh perspective, and enhance your creativity.

20. GET a basketball net for your trashcan and have a quick game while you formulate solutions to a puzzling situation. Invite a coworker to join you.

21. GIVE your team members bubble gum and have a bubble-blowing contest.

22. INVITE a juggler to your office to teach you and your coworkers how to juggle. You will laugh a lot, feel invigorated, and more playful. Creativity evolves from playing with ideas. Add a sense of play to your work environment.

While Stuck in Traffic or Waiting in Line:

1. DON'T FIGHT situations you can't change. Being stuck in traffic, a slowly moving line, or waiting for a plane to take off are not reasons to become stressed out. Raising your blood pressure, grinding your teeth, or tightly constricting your muscles will only make it harder to relax and sleep later on. Your health is too important to compromise this way! Instead, honor your body by engaging in deep breathing and repeating affirmations such as, "I move through life with ease. I go with the flow. I easily handle whatever challenges life presents. I am at peace." Don't waste your precious energy or risk your health fighting situations over which you have no control.

2. TAKE OFF your watch. It won't get you to your destination or through the line any sooner to be continually consulting your watch.

3. LISTEN to motivational audiotapes or CD's, or listen to an audiotaped book you've wanted to read. You can also do this while driving to and from work or while running errands. Borrow tapes or CD's from the public library.

4. EXERCISE your arms with a weight. (One arm at a time, of course!)

5. TIGHTEN your buttocks, your thighs, and your stomach to get in some isometric exercise.

6. **VISUALIZE** one of your goals becoming a reality. What do you do step-by-step to achieve it?

7. **PLAY** your favorite music.

8. **ENJOY** the silence, particularly if you've had a demanding day. Silence is a sweet, healing respite.

9. Gail Howerton, the CEO (Chief Energizing Officer) of Fun*cilitators, suggests that you put on a red clown nose and blow bubbles out of your car window. Sound like fun? To get your own big red nose contact Gail@funcilitators.com.

10. **BUY** some outrageous sunglasses that make you smile. Put them on and become a movie star evading the paparazzi.

11. **CHEW** gum really fast. This changes your focus *and* improves your breath.

12. To help pare down clutter, I cut articles that I want to read out of magazines and toss the rest. Then I put them in a folder in my purse. That way I can read the articles while waiting for appointments or riding in the car.

13. **FINGER** a string of worry beads (or a worry stone or a stress ball) to release tension when stuck in situations beyond your control. Slowly finger each bead before moving on to the next. Concentrate on the size, shape, and texture of each bead. This change in focus will help you alleviate muscular tension and achieve a calmer state.

Other Stress Busters:

1. **TRY** taking a different route to and from work periodically.

2. **KICK BACK!** Put on your pajamas right after dinner, and give yourself the rest of the evening off. No chores, no deadlines, no responsibilities, please! Put your feet up and **RELAX**.

3. HAVE a picnic on your living room floor.

4. Spend a few minutes each day pretending you are on vacation. THINK *vacation thoughts* and relax!

5. TURN OFF the television and talk. (Don't try this during the Super Bowl!)

6. SLEEP LATE, or at least linger in bed relaxing for a few extra minutes.

7. TAKE A BREAK from watching the evening news. It's typically depressing and stressful. Give your mind the evening off.

8. DO some mending, sew on buttons or do some type of needlework. The repetitive actions involved, for example in cross-stitching, are soothing to your mind, body and soul.

9. HAVE a romantic interlude. Sex is a proven (and fun!) stress reliever.

10. RELAX with a hot pack or heating pad on the spot in your body where you carry tension.

11. DO the *Macarena*.

12. INTERSPERSE breaks into running errands. Take a breather from your chores by stopping at a park or some other spot that you enjoy.

13. TURN OFF or UNPLUG the phone during dinner and devote your full attention to your loved ones.

14. When a favorite song comes on in the grocery store, grab your spouse or significant other and do a quick **DANCE** down the aisle. Dawne Brooks Gulla, Managing Partner of the Gulla Group, says this helps energize her when doing one of her less than favorite chores. These impromptu dances make Dawne and her husband, Frank, laugh and enjoy their task, as well as bringing smiles to the faces of other shoppers.

15. SPEND a few quiet minutes rocking in a quiet, dark room.

Time to Play Hooky?   51

16. PLAY a musical instrument.

17. CREATE your own doorway garden for a soothing, pleasant homecoming. Kathie Hightower suggests that you, "Create the best entryway possible to welcome you home each day. I started with one flowerpot last year. This year I have five. There is something wonderful about coming home to an inviting doorway" (p.53). This is just one of the many joys that Kathie recommends in her book *Simple Joys: Little Things That Make a BIG Difference*. To order call Quick Study Press at (703) 931-3620.

18. USE TV as an escape *only* if you are interested in the programs. Uninteresting shows create a low-level boredom that is actually tension-inducing according to Paul Wilson the author of *Instant Calm*.

> The rationale behind all of these suggestions is to give yourself short recovery periods to break away from your everyday, goal-driven routine, and to detoxify your system of the cumulative negative effects of stress and overexertion.

19. PREPARE for a visit from Mr. Sandman with a soothing, wind-down period. In her book *Magic Moments*, Kim Goad suggests that you "Practice before-bedtime rituals that help you relax or lull you to sleep. Read romantic novels or poetry, pray, or listen to soothing music" (p. 24). Perhaps a warm bath might relax you and wash away the tension of the day. Turn down the lights and enjoy. It's best to have an hour to unwind before you go to bed. This transition will help you reverse the physical and emotional states of arousal that your body and mind acquire daily, and help you sleep more soundly. (Note: NEVER watch the news *right* before bedtime. It's too unsettling.)

20. INDULGE in a long, nurturing hug.

21. PET your animals. Studies indicate that stroking a furry friend automatically reduces your blood pressure.

22. RELAX in a sauna or Jacuzzi to ease tense tired muscles.

52   PRACTICE SAFE STRESS!

What other stress busting breaks can you think of? What would rejuvenate and energize you? What would provide a brief escape from the madness of daily life? Restoration and refreshment are your goals. The rationale behind all of these suggestions is to give yourself short *recovery periods* to break away from your everyday, goal-driven routine, and to detoxify your system of the cumulative negative effects of stress and overexertion. During these recovery periods, the brain tends to transmit calming alpha waves and the body repairs and renews itself physiologically.

Listen to your body! Don't ignore its natural signals that it's time to play hooky. Loss of concentration, errors in your work, yawning, hunger, a drop in energy, daydreaming, boredom, memory problems, and mood swings are all signals for rejuvenation. Decrease your stress and increase your energy by taking a break.

Breaks help us clear out the cobwebs, fuel our energy, and provide a healthy release. Experiment with making specific breaks a part of your daily routine, i.e., routinely do neck rolls and shoulder shrugs while waiting at the copier or fax machine.

Productivity, enthusiasm, and vigor are grounded in play, not work. Don't wait for your next week long vacation to escape from the pressures of your job and your life. Work at play, play at work. Take a breather. Go play hooky for a few minutes!

11 • Run Away From Home

"For a needed respite, take a day off and tell everyone you're going out of town. Instead, spend the day at home...watching the latest Tom Cruise video, finishing that novel, or baking bread from scratch."

-Kim Goad
Magic Moments

When we were children, my brother would periodically threaten to run away from home. He got out a bandana, wrapped up his most prized possessions, and attached them to a stick for his getaway. I'm not certain where he got the stick and bandana idea. Perhaps watching *Spanky and Our Gang,* or *Lassie,* or some cowboy movie, but it seemed essential to his big escape.

I was not as adventurous. Whenever I felt like running away from home, I would go to my own special place and hide out from the world. That space was behind the sofa in the living room. Even as a child I hated to be cold or uncomfortable in any way, so I would never *really* run away from home. A quiet retreat was all I needed to sort through how the world was treating me and to look at my needs from the inside out.

This spot behind our sofa became my refuge in times of stress and confusion, when I had gotten into trouble, when I was mad at somebody, when I had had my feelings hurt, etc.

My private retreat proved a great way to revive myself whenever I was worn out from dealing with the world. Time in my own personal retreat refreshed my soul, enabled me to regain my inner calm and feel centered once again.

> Time in my own personal retreat refreshed my soul, enabled me to regain my inner calm and feel centered once again.

Our Christmas guests left yesterday, and I am ready to crawl behind the sofa. I love spending time with family and friends celebrating the holidays, but enough is enough. I admit it; I'm exhausted! I need a secluded sanctuary to hide away in for a while and unwind after the hectic holiday pace.

As we grow up, our problems and challenges become bigger too. Running away from home needs to be expanded to several hours, several days or even a week in order for us to fully evaluate our current situation, relax and wind down, recharge, and formulate a strategy for action.

My friend Susan runs away from home, in the figurative sense, every Saturday. She schedules nothing. These are her days to garden, read, whatever she desires. She may retreat to her home office, but she doesn't answer the phone or respond to faxes. There are no bells or whistles unless *she* decides to ring or blow them. Her family knows to disturb her *only* if there is an emergency, otherwise she is free from all encumbrances. This is her recovery day to totally disconnect from business and the world if she chooses. She creates an island of peace and serenity. She envelops herself with tranquility.

In the delightful book *Magic Moments: A Busy Woman's Guide to Forgotten Pleasures*, Kim Goad suggests that you make retreats a regular part of your annual routine. "Right now, take out your calendar and block off time within the next six months for vacations, long weekends, and special splurges. By planning ahead, you'll take control of your schedule—instead of vice versa" (p. 203).

I like that proactive approach! I am a planner and if it is written on my appointment book, I get it done. However, I have found that I need *extra space* in my calendar because many activities seem to take longer than I anticipate. Why not include space for running away from home? I can't always *find* an entire weekend as Goad suggests, but I can periodically *set aside* a day in advance.

Now it's your turn! When will you run away from home? What would replenish you? What soothing respite do you desire? Is it a mini-cation for pleasurable reading and napping? Exploring the placid, restive countryside? Do you need goal-setting time? A combination of the above? Get out your calendar and mark off time right now, or, better yet, grab your bandana and start packing.

12 · A Change of Pace

"Do I want my life to be a walk in the park, a jog in the park, or a rat race?"

-Fred Reever

Have you noticed how the pace of life seems to be escalating? More and more demands are made of us, and the expectation is that we meet those demands at a faster and faster pace. The individuals that I coach have crushing schedules and competing deadlines both at work and at home. They report feeling like lab rats, running through life's maze as fast as they possibly can. Rush, rush, rush. The pace is frantic!

This hurry to achieve can become a *constant* in our lives and, without us even being aware of it, we become habitual hurriers. I enjoy watching people, and I've noticed this sense of urgency played out in many forms in waiting rooms. Some people are forever in motion; relentlessly racing. They find it difficult to sit still, preferring instead to pace agitatedly back and forth as they wait to begin an appointment. Others nervously swing their crossed legs, tap their fingers and/or their feet. Fidgeting seems pervasive. It's as if the waiting room is filled with rush addicts, trying to squeeze one more thing into their already crammed schedules.

I want to say to these people, "Hey, even *if* you win the rat race you are still a rat! Is that how you choose to live your life? Do you want life to zoom by in a blur?" I prefer to focus upon the words of Eddie Cantor, "Slow down and enjoy life. It's not only the scenery you miss by going too fast - you also miss the sense of where you are going and why."

> "Hey, even if you win the rat race you are still a rat! Do you want your life to zoom by in a blur?"

How do you cope with life's accelerated pace, and the accompanying demands on your time and energy? Are you aware of the pace at which you move? Speak? Eat? Think? Work? Drive? Exercise? Does that pace vary? Sometimes fast, sometimes moderate, sometimes slower?

Are you stuck at one pace? Is that pace comfortable for you? Would you like to speed up? Slow down? At what pace do you *thrive* versus merely surviving? What is your *preferred* pace?

A silent, inner metronome that defines our pace and sets the rhythm of life guides each of us. Listen to your metronome. Become consciously aware of your pace. Find the rate that is the most comfortable and rewarding for you. Is it a walk in the park, a jog in the park, or a rat race? How might you vary that pace? Varying your pace will give you a breather to re-energize. It's up to you. What do you choose?

Give yourself permission to experiment with a change of pace. Remember Gandhi's wise words, "There is more to life than increasing its speed." Downshift a little and enjoy of life!

13 · It's Naptime!

"I usually take a two hour nap from 1-4."

-Yogi Berra

Remember being required to take a nap every afternoon at school? We would pull out our cushioned sleep pads and lie down for a revitalizing snooze. Sometimes we would even have milk and cookies afterwards. What a pleasant way to spend part of the afternoon!

That agreeable afternoon ritual was based upon what scientists have called the *post-lunch dip* in alertness that occurs whether or not food has been consumed. According to Dr. William Dement of the Sleep Disorders Clinic at Stanford University, it seems nature intended adults to nap in the middle of the day due to our natural biphasic sleep pattern. The same drop in core body temperature and alertness that causes us to fall asleep at night occurs on a slightly smaller scale in the afternoon. No wonder our energy level decreases, we get drowsy, and find it hard to concentrate and function at full capacity in the afternoon!

Sleep specialist, Dr. James B. Maas recommends a 15 to 30 minute nap to help you feel refreshed, and to overcome sleep deprivation. In his book *POWER Sleep,* Dr. Maas states that due to our 24-hour society, nearly everyone is sleep deprived.

Sleep deprivation lowers the immune system's ability to fight off viral infections, makes us irritable, causes untold mistakes and accidents, decreases our ability to be creative and impairs our judgment, as well as creating greater susceptibility to heart attacks and gastrointestinal disorders. Maas believes that naps should hold the same revered status as daily exercise because they positively impact wellness.

Maas also points out that sleep debt is not reduced by artificial stimulants, so why not get some much-needed sleep? His prescription for overcoming sleep deprivation is "Take a nap" (p. 108). I continue to value naps, and can think of no better way to spend part of a Saturday or Sunday afternoon than by recharging my mind and body. Napping brings on a feeling beyond compare! Remember, 15 to 30 minutes are ideal. Longer naps may leave you feeling groggy and sluggish or interfere with your ability to sleep through the night.

> Due to our 24-hour society, nearly everybody is sleep deprived today, and naps should be elevated to the same high status as daily exercise because they positively impact wellness.

During the workweek naps are not a practical reality for most of us, even though some forward thinking organizations recognize the value of naps and have set up nap rooms for their employees. If your organization has not yet begun to appreciate the power of naps, consider resting your mind through creative visualization, meditation, writing in your journal, a brief walk, or gentle stretching exercises to help perk you up during the afternoon slump.

Listen to your body! Monitor your downtime and do not schedule important meetings during that slump that generally occurs between 2 and 5pm. If meetings can not be avoided during your afternoon lull, experiment with ways to refresh yourself before the meeting begins.

So now you have it. Naps produce a health benefit in addition to making us feel and look better. Want to feel more alert, dynamic, and full of energy? Go take a nap. Sweet dreams! Milk and cookies are optional.

14. Tickle Your Fancy

"What soap is to the body, laughter is to the soul."

-Yiddish Proverb

I am very fortunate to still have my 94 year-old Granny. Granny is almost 4'9" with her shoes on, and she weighs about 80 pounds. It's no surprise that my Mom nicknamed her "Bug" because of her diminutive size.

Granny Bug's spirit is anything but diminutive. She told me on the telephone one day that she needed to go because she was scheduled "to help the *old, sick* people in the Care Center play Bingo" at the Masonic Home where she lives. This made me laugh because Granny was a youngster of 90 at this time, and her words have continued to stick with me. She remains young at heart, playful, and loves to laugh despite her advanced youth.

> Laughter seems to be an important factor when looking at longevity. Is that because laughter reduces stress, and stress is a killer?

Granny and her friends have great stories to tell about what happens to the residents at the Masonic Home. One of my favorites was when she and a number of the other residents went to pay their last respects to someone who had passed away. Elmer, the new guy on the block, had moved in earlier that week, and he was trying hard to fit in. He decided to join the group and pay his respects as well.

Elmer's (the name has been changed because Granny is hoping to get lucky) eyesight is not what it used to be, and he some how got separated from the group. Everyone had visited their departed friend and was back in the van ready to return to their home. Everyone EXCEPT Elmer that is, so the driver went inside to find him. Elmer was found attending the funeral of *someone else*. Someone he did *not* know!

> **Laughter is an internal messsage.**

They all had a good laugh about this, and it was Elmer who told me this story. As he recounted his adventure, we all got a case of the giggles! How refreshing to find someone so good humored, who can laugh at himself and continues to enjoy every second of life. His sense of humor must have helped him reach age 95.

Laughter seems to be an important factor when looking at longevity. Bob Hope, the King of Comedy, was born in 1903 and is still making people laugh. George Burns lived to be almost 100 years young. Red Skelton lived to be well into his 80's. Comedians live forever. Is that because laughter reduces stress, and stress is a killer?

Yes! Peter McLaughlin points out that, "Levity, in fact, demolishes negative stress, being incompatible with it psychologically and physiologically" (*Catchfire*, p. 199). Laughter is a tremendous stress buster, and you are improving your health in the process. Laughter releases health-producing, calming hormones, as well as slowing the heart rate, lowering blood pressure, and encouraging deep breathing. It has a rejuvenating quality; a restorative effect upon your body, mind, and soul. Laughter is an internal massage.

Are you living an overly serious life? How can you evoke unbridled laughter? Perhaps you'll want to go to a comedy club, get a joke book and surprise your friends and family with a joke a day, or get on an email joke chain (my friend Mike sends me jokes almost daily). Or visit a card store and read funny cards for a few laughs. You might start a bulletin board where you and your colleagues, or family, post funny cartoons or start a humor library decorated with humorous posters and filled with books, toys, audio and video tapes that make you laugh.

Why not scatter laugh triggers throughout your home and office? I recently bought myself a Mickey Mouse toothbrush that makes me smile every time I use it. I've also got a pair of bouncing eyeball glasses beside my computer that I can don whenever I need to laugh and gain a creative perspective.

Set a new goal. Lighten up! That famous philosopher Anonymous said, "Laughter is like changing a baby's diaper - it doesn't permanently solve any problems, but it makes things more acceptable for a while." Might life become more agreeable, playful, and fun if *you* smiled and laughed more?

15. Time Out

"He who knows others is wise; he who knows himself is enlightened."

-Lao-Tzu

When I was in elementary school there were times when I would much rather talk to my friends than get my work completed, and as a result, my teacher asked me to stand in the corner. During such "time outs" my classmates and I were encouraged to think about what we had done, and contemplate how we could become better students in the future.

I tended to enjoy using these time outs (this happened quite often) to think about recess, drawing, going to the library, or whatever came to me at the moment. Now I realize what a gift my teacher provided me. The concept of time out—to be alone, a time for quiet reflection, to focus, and get in touch with my own priorities is something I still yearn for and create on a daily basis. It's nice to be alone and explore my thoughts . . . to enjoy *me!*

My favorite time of the day is early morning when the world is fresh and new again, ripe with possibilities. I enjoy my time out to luxuriate in the early morning silence, and to recharge my body, mind and soul for the day ahead. I use this quiet, alone time to get in touch myself from the inside out. I create my own contemplative corner.

Time outs are especially beneficial during a busy day when multiple demands and priorities are pulling you in various directions. A few quiet moments alone, spent focusing on your inner needs are rejuvenating. Time out will help you reconnect with your self and your soul, and help you regain a sense of well being and control. A time out serves as an oasis for the spirit. Make a space on your calendar *each day* for a time out.

To create a time out, find a secluded conference room or close your office door. If you work at home find a quiet, private place for your time out. Get earplugs if necessary to shut out distractions. Enjoy the silence! Practice some yoga stretches, relaxation exercises, or meditate for 15 or 20 minutes during lunchtime. A Zen alarm clock with an exquisite, mellow chime to call you back to the world may be a good investment to make your time out special. Or if the weather is nice, escape to the out of doors and appreciate nature's abundant natural beauty as you walk or relax during your lunch break.

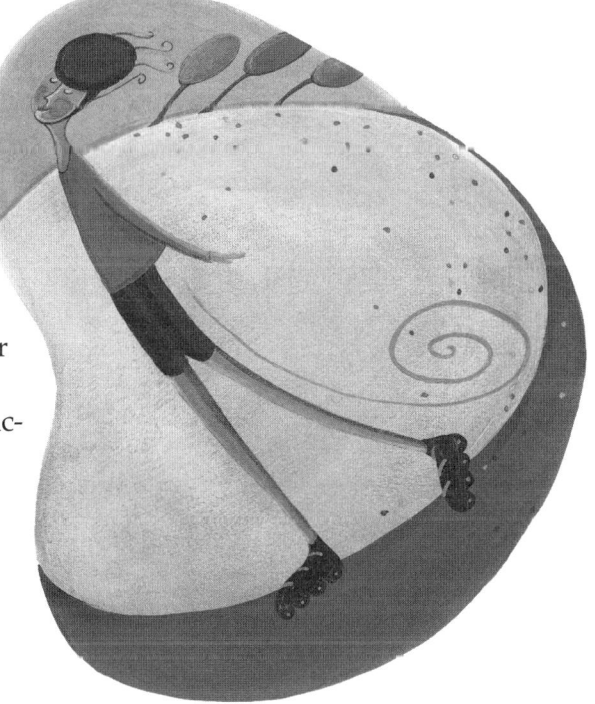

What type of time outs help you feel centered and focused? Some people prefer inspirational reading, others t'ai chi, prayer, or peaceful walks. Time outs are a great way to revive your spirit. Experiment to see what works best for you. Give yourself permission to take a time out and be alone today. Go stand in the corner if you have to!

> The concept of time out—to be alone, a time for quiet reflection, to focus, and get in touch with my own priorities is something I still yearn for and create on a daily basis.

16 · You Don't Have to Cook a Turkey

"Save your energy to put towards things
which give you pleasure, instead of driving
yourself crazy with minutiae."

-Gail Howerton
Hit Any Key To Energize:
A Caffeine-Free Guide To Perk Up Your Spirits

Does hearing the word "Thanksgiving" conjure up images of an energizing, peaceful, joyful celebration for you, *or* does it remind you of running a race where the finish line keeps being moved farther and farther away? Thanksgiving, as well as other holiday celebrations, is meant to commemorate daily life, our families, and being together, *not* to drive us to a state of exhaustion.

How have you traditionally celebrated Thanksgiving? Do you totally clean your house? Have the carpets professionally decontaminated? Retouch soiled walls with paint? Decorate for the season? Cook for weeks or days ahead of time? Starch and iron the tablecloths and napkins? Polish the silver? Drag out the fine china? Develop a seating chart? Design place cards for each of your guests? Make Granny's renowned rolls? Create floral centerpieces? And become so tired and stressed out that by the time your family and friends arrive that you don't enjoy their visit?

That sounds like a prison sentence to me, not a celebration! I fell into the trap of attempting to create the idyllic, June Clever holiday feast for a number of years. Finally, I woke up and realized that even though traditions are passed down from generation to generation we have a *choice* regarding which traditions we would *like* to continue and which we have outgrown. We have the ability to choose among options and to act with a measure of freedom. We can create new traditions that fit our current lifestyle and our busy lives.

> Let this holiday season mark the end of unnecessary errands, compulsive cleaning, and any other needless tasks leading to overwork and exhaustion.

One Thanksgiving we relaxed and enjoyed a simple buffet of finger foods such as ham and turkey biscuits, deviled eggs, pumpkin tarts purchased from a local bakery (preparing wonderful foods is their *full-time job* and they are experts. Why not let them help out with the celebration?), etc. You get the idea. My Grandmother commented on how nice it was to be able to sit and talk, rather than me being tied up in the kitchen, *away* from my family.

Last year we spent Thanksgiving in the Bahamas. Ordering pina coladas beside the pool is my idea of giving thanks! Send your family and friends words of Thanksgiving on postcards. Holidays are supposed to be celebrations, not self-created prisons or drudgery.

Experiment with new *traditions* until you find out what works best for you. Perhaps you'd like for Thanksgiving to be a potluck this year, where everyone helps by bringing a dish. For an easy clean up your guests could take their own containers home to be washed. One friend of mine experimented by using festively decorated paper plates, napkins, cups, and disposable flatware. She's hooked! Everyone tossed his or her used dishes, and all that was left to do was run the trash compactor. She's vowed to never go back to using the good china again for holiday feasts.

Perhaps your family might like to put together a food basket for the needy. There are many options from which to choose! How would you *like* to celebrate Thanksgiving? Christmas? Hanukkah? If you *enjoy* cooking, great! Do it. Otherwise, ask your family for their ideas. Maybe there is *one thing or activity* that makes that day special for each of them. For my brother, it is my sweet potato, peach, and pecan casserole. Knowing that, I can focus on *only* the treats that delight my family, rather than preparing a multi-course feast that has no special meaning to anyone.

Let this holiday season mark the end of unnecessary errands, compulsive cleaning, and any other needless tasks leading to overwork and exhaustion. Vow to never again greet your guests feeling like a wind up toy nearly at its end. What would bring you *pleasure* this Thanksgiving? How could you have more energy to enjoy yourself? How could you feel more relaxed and calm during the holidays? This year, make it your goal to celebrate in a stress-free manner that enables you to lighten up, smile, celebrate, and experience the joy of the season.

17 • Are You the Manager of Your Universe?

"What are the conditions under which it is possible for me to be whole?"

-Richard J. Leider
Life Skills

Before I began focusing on *not* overworking and underplaying, Bart used to call me the "Manager of the Universe." I was an overly responsible perfectionist, always giving so much to clients, associates, and the community that I had little left over to give to those I love *or* to myself.

Now, instead of managing the *entire* universe, I focus on small, positive things that I can do to create the conditions that make *my unique portion* of the universe more nurturing and pleasant. For example, I have significantly cut down on my caffeine intake, yet in my travels I kept finding that many restaurants and airlines do not serve decaffeinated or herbal teas. A simple solution for creating the conditions that make me feel whole is to carry a few of my favorite decaffeinated tea bags with me.

Or when on planes or trains I find it helpful to take my mini-sound system so that, if need be, I can put on my earphones and listen to soothing music as I work or read. That way I can drown out fellow passengers with megaphone voices, which carry from the very back to the front of the plane, or the cries of unhappy children. I manage my small part of the universe without becoming tense. I can remain focused by eliminating outside distractions.

Another way that I create the conditions that make me feel whole is to keep a five pound weight in my car for traffic jams. As I sit in the "parking lot" that some roadways become, I exercise my biceps and triceps. This helps me manage stress *and* avoid flabby upper arms. (Did I mention that I have had a phobia about upper arm flab since my early years when some of my teachers would write on the blackboard? The image of their exposed upper arms jiggling like a dimpled bowl of lemon Jello is permanently burned into my memory. It was not a pretty sight!) Now traffic jams are *almost* welcomed so I can do something good for me.

> Instead of managing the entire universe, I focus on small, positive things that I can do to create the conditions that make my universe more nurturing and pleasant.

What small steps could you take to more effectively manage your unique portion of the universe? Try to list at least ten. This week try out one small step to create a more nurturing environment for yourself, an environment that makes you feel whole.

18. "To Do" or "Not To Do"... That is the Question

"Without a deadline, baby, I wouldn't do nothing."

-Duke Ellington

Many of my clients seem to operate from the *heap on syndrome*, pushing themselves to get more and more things done in less and less time. They trade in their ability to enjoy the present for a to-do list that never ends.

> **Shorter to-do lists add up to less stress and more time to enjoy each day.**

As a matter of fact, one of my clients has a running joke with his wife about her *many* to-do lists. Fred says that he is going to bury Mary with her hands full of her lists. Like Mary, you will die with a to-do list, but will you die feeling successful and happy, or frustrated and tired? Will you have missed life in the process of *doing*?

Bart and I have been good influences on one another where lists are concerned. I *used* to get up every morning and make to detailed list of all the things I wanted to get done that day. Then I would systematically proceed to *push* myself through these exhausting lists, crossing off item after item until I had completed each and every one.

Bart took a different approach. He would look at his list and ask himself, "How many of these items can I put off until tomorrow?" and then he would cross off item after item until his list seemed manageable, or as he says, "The only good list is a *shorter* list."

We have both moderated our approaches to improve our effectiveness. I strive to be more gentle with myself so that I can *enjoy* parts of each day, and Bart no longer deletes as much from his list. (He has been known to *lose* a list or two though.)

Are you so caught up in the *outcome* of activities and getting everything done that you do not allow yourself to enjoy the *process*? Is it time to reassess your approach to to-do lists? Make a list of all of the advantages of *losing* that list (trust me, there *are* advantages). Ask your children, your spouse or significant other, and your best friend to help you come up with advantages to losing your lists, especially if you are having difficulty coming up with any. (Be careful here in case they are *list addicts* also!)

Does your approach to to-do lists support or hinder your ability to enjoy the present moment? How do you want to modify your approach? Experiment, but remember where lists are concerned *less is more!* Shorter to-do lists add up to *less* stress and *more* time to enjoy each day.

19. A Talk with Your Imaginary Friend

"I began these pages for myself, in order to think out my own particular pattern of living, my own individual balance of life, work and human relationships. And since I think best with a pencil in my hand, I started naturally to write."

-Anne Morrow Lindbergh
Gift from the Sea

Growing up, when it seemed as if no one in the entire world could understand me, I would talk with my imaginary friend, Becky. Becky never interrupted me. She always listened patiently, waiting for me to figure out and articulate exactly what was troubling me. I always felt better after Becky let me ramble through my thoughts, and finally pinpoint the source of my discontent.

Today, instead of talking to Becky, I write in my journal. Writing my thoughts down is a centering ritual that helps me clear my overcrowded mind. It serves as a mental cleansing, much as my early talks with Becky did. Writing calms the 300-ring circus of my jumbled mind.

Sometimes writing in my journal comes readily and easily. At other times, it starts out as a "laundry list" to be tackled today rather than inspired insights that enlighten and fortify. I get in touch with and process my feelings, fine tune my thoughts, or work out ideas or solutions to problems in my journal. My journal helps me become grounded and centered. It opens the door to my soul and helps me regain a sense of control over my life.

Writing in my journal is a great stress reliever. It enables me to take my churning whirlwind of thoughts, worries, and ideas and make them concrete, visible, and manageable. Whirling nebulous worries loom as large, frightening and menacingly as those monsters that used to lurk under my bed during childhood. These scary worry-monsters seem to know when I am most vulnerable, for example in the middle of the night, and that's when they choose to pounce. Yet when brought out into the light they lose their power and intensity, and seem less frightening when clearly articulated and captured on paper.

> **Writing my thoughts down is a centering ritual that helps me clear my overcrowded mind.**

Capturing my thoughts on paper also stops my mind from spinning and wasting unnecessary energy. Emptying my mind helps me attain clarity of thought and develop a clear course of action rather than merely spinning my wheels worrying. I emerge from writing in my journal in a much more *orderly* state of mind.

My journal serves as a comforting sanctuary, which enables me to sort through emotional clutter and emerge cleansed, ready to face the world. Might a journal comfort you and help you feel centered? Fifteen to twenty minutes is all it takes. Why not try keeping a journal and experience the peace of mind it can provide. *Your* imaginary friend is patiently waiting to listen to you!

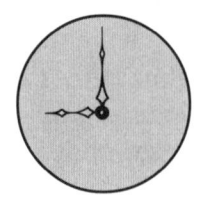

20 • Beat the Clock

"Let time be your friend and not a constant opponent."

-Loretta LaRoche
Relax-You May Only Have a Few Minutes Left

Recruiters and their managers work in a fast-paced world. Employers want temporary staff members on board *yesterday*. Working on short notice is the name of the game. In order to make money as a recruiter, you are either on the phone interviewing and placing people or talking to employers seeking job leads. Time is money. Recruiters are continually battling the ticking away of the seconds, the hours, and the days. They live by the clock.

My friend Billie, who worked her way up to become a District Manager for a national recruiting firm, lived by the clock. Her days were filled with deadlines, long hours, and high stress. I often wondered how Billie maintained her positive attitude, high spirits and remained playful and energetic with such a demanding job. As I got to know Billie better, I discovered that she has a secret that helped her thrive in this pressure filled, time-oriented environment.

Billie's secret was to escape the everyday, "nine-to-five" (does *anyone* just work from nine-to-five?) routine and create a respite from reality. After shedding her sensible business suit and

Beat the Clock   77

pumps for her comfortable walking clothes and Reeboks, she also sheds one more important workplace symbol - her watch.

Shedding her watch is a ritual Billie still uses today as a signal that she is off from work and it is *time* (pardon the pun) to relax. I admire her ability to set clear boundaries to protect her personal time. Shedding her watch is a personal time protector.

Billie and I have been fortunate enough to work on a number of projects together lately and I can't tell you how many mornings I have seen her strap on her watch as I drove us to our work site. Her action even began to say to me, "It is time to switch into work mode." What an effective time delineator!

How do you draw the line between work and personal time? What would help you disconnect from work? Do you have a ritual to celebrate the end of work and the beginning of the rest of your life?

If your life is filled with timetables, you are due an escape into timelessness. Loosen up! Explore the joys of spontaneity. How might you beat the clock? Could taking off your watch be something you could do for even *part* of a day, perhaps on the weekend, to remind yourself to relax and become a human being instead of a human *doing*? How will you befriend time?

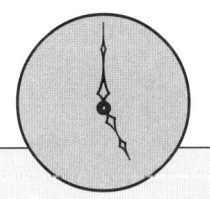

> Do you have a ritual to celebrate the end of work and the beginning of the rest of your life?

Make Fun of Life!

PART 3

21 · Recapture the Delight of Recess

"Would the child you once were
be proud of the adult you are today?"

- Walt Disney

Remember the feeling you got when it was time to go outside for recess? Recess was an exhilarating respite when my mind, heart, and body were fully engaged in the present moment. I was FREE! Recess was a time to focus on play and delight, and I didn't have to be quiet if I didn't want to! Recess was a hiatus from my childhood job—the pursuit of learning. We laughed frequently, sang, and played with carefree abandon.

According to Webster, play means "to move lightly, to frolic." Are you having enough fun in your life? How much do you move lightly, play, and frolic? Consider the following activities. Which did you enjoy taking part in as a child? Put a check beside each of those enjoyable activities.

- ☐ watching clouds and identifying animals in them
- ☐ telling ghost stories
- ☐ collecting frog eggs and watching them turn into tadpoles

- playing musical chairs
- swinging
- playing follow the leader
- skipping
- coloring
- watching it rain from your screened porch
- blowing bubbles
- running through the sprinkler to cool off
- playing croquet
- dressing up and going to a Halloween party
- shooting pool
- putting on plays
- bobbing for apples
- helping bake and decorate Christmas cookies
- playing Bingo®
- watching *The Three Stooges®*
- looking into a kaleidoscope
- playing with Gumby® and Pokey®
- riding a carousel
- reading comic books
- making a "tent" with one of Mom's sheets and camping out under the stars
- touring a fire station and seeing the fire engines
- playing school
- buying ice cream from a vendor
- having your face painted by a clown
- bouncing up and down on a bed

Recapture the Delight of Recess 83

- ❑ playing with balloons
- ❑ riding a hobby horse
- ❑ playing kickball
- ❑ drawing
- ❑ playing Simon Says
- ❑ rolling in the grass
- ❑ going to the airport to watch the planes take off and land
- ❑ playing with clay
- ❑ singing
- ❑ playing dodge ball
- ❑ making ice cream out of snow
- ❑ dancing
- ❑ playing with pets
- ❑ jumping rope
- ❑ playing catch
- ❑ making s'mores
- ❑ sailing sticks down a stream
- ❑ playing "Horse" with a basketball
- ❑ doing the limbo
- ❑ riding a coin-operated mechanical horse or race car
- ❑ playing the card game Fish®
- ❑ tasting the sweet nectar of honeysuckle
- ❑ climbing trees
- ❑ playing crab soccer
- ❑ watching cartoons
- ❑ playing with a Slinky®

Recapture the Delight of Recess   85

- ☐ flying kites
- ☐ playing tag
- ☐ roasting marshmallows
- ☐ playing hide and seek
- ☐ setting up and running a "grocery store"
- ☐ playing Ring Around the Rosy
- ☐ going Trick or Treating
- ☐ reading Nancy Drew and/or Hardy Boys novels
- ☐ bouncing a ball against the house and catching it
- ☐ playing Dominoes®
- ☐ searching for seashells
- ☐ playing 20 Questions
- ☐ dancing around the May pole
- ☐ carving jack-o-lanterns
- ☐ playing a kazoo
- ☐ building forts
- ☐ having parades and inviting the neighbors to watch
- ☐ playing connect-a-dot
- ☐ dressing up in grown up's clothes
- ☐ playing Crazy 8's®
- ☐ doing the Hokey Pokey
- ☐ playing Twister®
- ☐ having family game night and playing together
- ☐ going to the rodeo
- ☐ having a slumber party
- ☐ giggling uncontrollably

> Are you having enough fun in your life? How often do you move lightly, play, and frolic?

MAKE FUN OF LIFE!

- ☐ playing Pick Up Sticks®
- ☐ rolling down hills
- ☐ drawing with an Etch-a-Sketch®
- ☐ playing records and having a sing-a-long or a dance party
- ☐ telling knock-knock jokes
- ☐ riding a scooter
- ☐ searching for four leaf clovers
- ☐ jumping up and down
- ☐ doing magic tricks
- ☐ making mud pies
- ☐ dressing up like cowboys/girls and riding the range
- ☐ riding bikes
- ☐ reading comic books
- ☐ raking a big pile of leaves and jumping in them
- ☐ playing Solitaire
- ☐ finger-painting
- ☐ collecting lightning bugs and putting them in a jar to watch their iridescent glow
- ☐ playing hopscotch
- ☐ roller skating
- ☐ playing Monopoly®
- ☐ playing Checkers®
- ☐ playing Yahtzee®
- ☐ playing Candyland®
- ☐ playing Operation®
- ☐ climbing on monkey bars at the playground

Recapture the Delight of Recess

- ☐ playing Chinese Checkers®
- ☐ taking ballet, tap and other dance lessons
- ☐ going for a walk
- ☐ swimming
- ☐ playing Parcheesi®
- ☐ going on an Easter egg hunt
- ☐ having a goldfish
- ☐ trying on treasures from your Grandmother's jewelry box
- ☐ going to the playground
- ☐ ice skating
- ☐ baking cookies
- ☐ playing baseball
- ☐ throwing a Frisbee®
- ☐ holding a buttercup under a friend's chin to see if it glowed
- ☐ playing volleyball
- ☐ searching for tree frogs and making them pets
- ☐ playing with dolls and stuffed animals
- ☐ cooking with your Easy-Bake Oven®
- ☐ playing Uno®
- ☐ going to story hour at the library
- ☐ playing Sorry®
- ☐ playing Trouble®
- ☐ painting by the numbers
- ☐ building model cars and planes

> It's refreshing to get lost in lovely memories of your youth and childhood pleasures.

MAKE FUN OF LIFE!

- ☐ playing charades
- ☐ throwing darts
- ☐ doing cartwheels
- ☐ juggling
- ☐ playing Red Rover
- ☐ riding bikes with *no hands*
- ☐ having a tea party
- ☐ reading your favorite book
- ☐ going on picnics
- ☐ having a snowball fight
- ☐ playing jacks
- ☐ having eraser relay races
- ☐ twirling a baton
- ☐ playing tug-of-war
- ☐ shooting marbles
- ☐ going for a sleigh ride
- ☐ playing the card game War
- ☐ putting on puppet shows
- ☐ riding a skateboard
- ☐ playing Kick the Can
- ☐ coloring and decorating Easter eggs
- ☐ building a tree house
- ☐ making snowmen (and women)
- ☐ playing with a yo-yo
- ☐ making snow angels
- ☐ playing Hang Man
- ☐ going shopping downtown with Mom

- ❐ playing tick-tack-toe
- ❐ climbing on a jungle gym
- ❐ playing Old Maid/Bachelor®
- ❐ swinging on tires hung from trees
- ❐ playing Clue®
- ❐ taking dolls for a walk in a baby carriage
- ❐ going to the State Fair

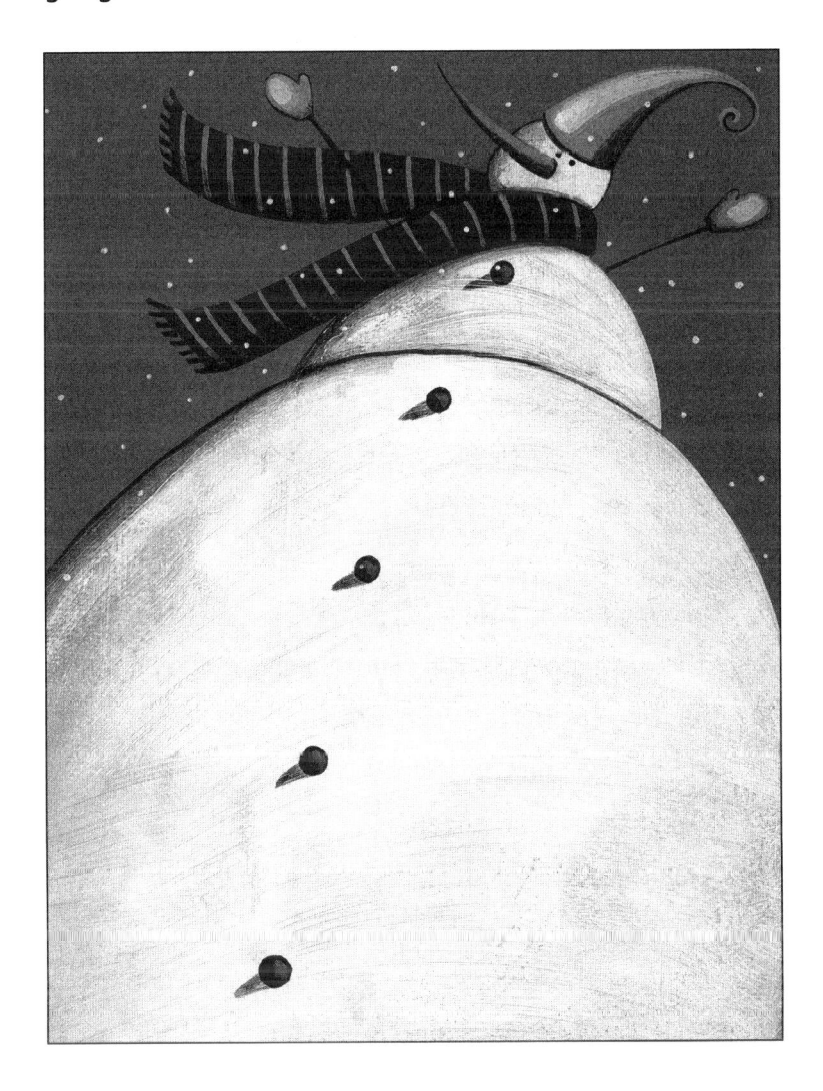

- ❒ going on a scavenger hunt
- ❒ playing in the sand box
- ❒ catching snow flakes on your tongue
- ❒ talking with your imaginary friend
- ❒ setting up a stand and selling lemonade
- ❒ walking in the rain and jumping in puddles
- ❒ going to the zoo
- ❒ digging for worms and going fishing
- ❒ walking on stilts
- ❒ playing with paper dolls
- ❒ whistling
- ❒ playing King of the Mountain
- ❒ going for piggy back rides
- ❒ playing Ping-Pong
- ❒ going to the circus
- ❒ putting funny faces on Mr. Potato Head®
- ❒ going to a magic show
- ❒ thumb wrestling
- ❒ playing badminton
- ❒ throwing a coin into a fountain and making a wish
- ❒ hunting for buried treasure
- ❒ collecting coins or stamps
- ❒ doing crossword puzzles
- ❒ playing with sparklers
- ❒ having a pillow fight
- ❒ going to the movies
- ❒ jumping on a trampoline

- ❏ playing with a hula hoop
- ❏ building with blocks or Legos®
- ❏ feeding ducks
- ❏ gliding down a sliding board
- ❏ going on hay rides
- ❏ building sandcastles
- ❏ making a wish on the first star of the evening
- ❏ looking for the pot of gold at the end of rainbows

Add your own favorites:

_____
_____
_____
_____
_____
_____

I bet you are smiling now after reading this list of childhood activities and thinking about your own playtime fun. It's refreshing to get lost in lovely memories of your youth and childhood pleasures. Looking at this list of activities, plus those that you added, are you surprised by the *number* of playful activities you engaged in as a child? *How many* playful, fun activities do you engage in *now*?

Ready for some lighthearted fun? It's time to come out and play! Which of these activities can you enjoy engaging in today? Or at least this week? What weren't you allowed to do as a child that you'd like to do now? What prevents you from doing that? Be mischievous! Try it anyway and notice the impact on your sense of well-being.

MAKE FUN OF LIFE!

Part of us grows up and part of us never does, so unleash your inner "fun-ster." Add more fun, merriment and delight to your life. You know you want to. The joy of childhood is only a few moments away. Go out for recess, kick up your heels and make *these* the "good old days."

> How many playful, fun activities do you engage in now?

22. Are We Having Fun Yet?

"Have fun! Misery is optional."

-Jean Wescott

How do you spell FUN? I spell it Focused, in an Unusual environment with No obligations.

How much of your time is spent in focused activities? By focused I mean engaging in ONE activity at a time, giving that *one* activity your undivided attention. I have a friend who can talk on the phone, sweep the floor, wash clothes, cook dinner, and make tomorrow's lunches for her family all at the same time. Much like a three-ring circus, many of the women I interact with think nothing of juggling three or four activities at once. This seems to be the time management strategy that busy women cultivate to get them through each day.

No fun here! Just lots of pressure to achieve. No focus or undivided attention either and *lots* of obligations. When I think of obligations I think of have to's, should's and ought's, not want to's. Want to's are energizing. Want to's are energy *gains*, not energy drains.

> **F**ocus on one activity
>
> **U**nusual environment
>
> **N**o obligations

Think back over the last week, what FUN activities did you engage in? As I think back to a FUN activity, Bart and I went out to brunch on Sunday. For that hour or so (OK it was two hours, we shared a bottle of champagne), we focused all of our attention upon each other, without distractions. There was no telephone or fax to interrupt us. There was no television vying for our attention. For a few moments we were able to get lost in each other. So Step 1 in the FUN equation is *focus*.

Step 2 in the FUN quest is to be in an *unusual environment*. An unusual environment is any place that you don't find yourself daily. For example, I love leisurely bubble baths, yet don't have time to take them most days. I usually opt for a quick shower instead, so my bathtub is an unusual environment for me. Your screened porch or deck might be unusual environments for you. Novelty is exhilarating, and we don't always have to go out or spend money to create that novelty or to go to an unusual place. Create an unusual environment *simply*—by adding candles, enjoyable music, aromatherapy, flowers, or by using your fine china.

> It's rejuvenating to take the weight of the world off of your shoulders periodically, and forget about responsibilities. Give yourself permission to have fun. Take a respite from adulthood, and practice being *irresponsible* even for a few moments.

The "N" in FUN stands for *no obligations* or responsibilities. While we were having brunch, the house wasn't calling out to be cleaned, the bills weren't calling out to be paid, and the pile of unread mail wasn't saying, "Read me!" For those few peaceful moments we had no obligations, responsibilities, or worries. We were able to escape from our normal routines and relax.

It's rejuvenating to take the weight of the world off of your shoulders periodically, and forget about responsibilities.

Give yourself permission to rest one day or part of a day. Recapture the carefree spirit of your childhood and have fun.

What would you like to do to bring more FUN into your life today? What do you *want* to do? Make a list of five want to's. Remember this list can only contain *pleasurable activities*, not product-producers or accomplishments. Your accomplishment will be enjoying the process, having FUN and relaxing.

What *unusual environment* will you select? It could be a park, a museum, or your own backyard. Remember that *focus* is the key. Turn your mind off to outside distractions, enjoy the novelty of being in an *unusual environment*, having *no obligations* and have FUN. During these few moments experience the pleasure of enjoyment. The pleasure will be intensified and even more exquisite if it's been a while since you let yourself go and have fun. Relish the escape!

> Escape from your normal routine and make FUN of life!

23 • Create a Feast for Your Senses

"How sense-luscious the world is."

-Diane Ackerman
A Natural History of the Senses

During a recent trip to Rome, I experienced sheer sensual delight in the Piazza Navona. It was a glorious Sunday afternoon, and the sheer beauty of the day added to our pleasure. The warm spring sunshine gently bathed our skin as we walked arm in arm at a leisurely pace.

The piazza vibrated with life. It was filled with amazingly beautiful sculpted fountains, artists showing their wares, people enjoying meals at the cafes, and strolling musicians. Periodically the patrons at the cafes would join the musicians in singing, and we heard lots of laughter. What a zest for enjoying life the Italians possess! They enjoy a gracious receptivity to life and truly live life with gusto.

There were colorful flowers everywhere, which served as a feast for our eyes. Flowers were housed in bountiful pots, in boxes on the porches and in the windows, and roof gardens tumbled gracefully over the sides of the buildings. They served as a sunsplashed celebration of color.

Many of the quaint old buildings were decorated with intricate wrought ironwork like you would see in New Orleans. Peaceful church bells called out occasionally. Water babbled from the three huge baroque fountains. We noticed the smell of spring in the air—all fresh and green. It was a festival of sights and sounds. My senses were saturated. What a sumptuous experience!

We delighted in the Old World charm, and took our time to enjoy a relaxing, unhurried lunch. The tastes of the light sauces were a sublime surprise after the "Italian" food I was accustomed to back home. The waiters and the Italian patrons were very warm, friendly and open. They always seem to welcome visitors with a smile. I appreciate their ability to live for and enjoy the moment. This experience will be an exquisite memory for a lifetime.

As we returned home, I began to experiment with ways to recapture those rich sensual feelings of zest, gusto and relaxation. For example, there is a colorful, little garden at a local wine bistro where we love to hold hands and enjoy a lingering Sunday brunch. We delight in savoring the tastes and textures of the food, basking in the warm glow of the sunshine, listening to the cheerful call of the birds, and relishing the flowers' perfumed fragrance.

Or there is a picnic spot beside a gently, rippling stream where ducks and their babies frolic, hoping to be fed. I take pleasure in listening to the softly gurgling water as I eat my lunch there, and last year thoroughly enjoyed watching the baby ducks grow with each visit. Jazz music is added to this enchanting patio scene on Friday nights. What a way to end the week!

> How might you satisy your hunger for life?

How might you experiment with adding a variety of sensual pleasures to your life? How might you satisfy your hunger for life? Why not add zest and gusto to your life and live a day, or parts of a day, like an Italian? What sumptuous sensations will you provide your eyes? Your ears? Your nose? Your taste buds? Your sense of touch? You can do this at home and/or at work. What would be exhilarating for you?

Dare to become a sensualist. Open the windows of your senses. Focus on enjoyment, and tasting life! Savor your world, and it's rich treasure chest of pleasures. Heed life's exhilarating sensations, and join in the feast.

24. All Work and No Play?

*"It is in his pleasure that a man really lives;
it is from his leisure that he constructs
the true fabric of self."*

-Agnes Repplier

Most of my clients can't tell me even *one* hobby or leisure activity in which they currently engage. I often hear, "I *used* to...paint, do needle work, bowl, refinish furniture, make pottery," etc. You fill in the blank. Very few use the present tense to respond to my inquiry.

What pastimes do you enjoy? I truly enjoy dance. It's fun and I love to take dance lessons. Much to Bart's dismay many of those lessons have been for couples, ranging from ballroom dancing, to swing, to… you name it! I've signed us up to learn how to do it.

While in Spain we went to see several flamingo dancing shows. What colorful, raucous experiences! My favorite was a show in Granada in the *Cueva de la Rocio,* a cave where gypsies actually live. (Bart made his flamingo dancing debut here, but that's another story!)

As you know flamingo dancers are very evocative and passionate. They concentrate so intensely as they dance that they appear to be in trance. Our guide, André explained to us that the best gypsy dancers are in touch with *"el duende"*, the little spirit or genie that lives inside of them as they are in this very focused state.

Each of us possess *el duende*. She is present any time we are totally focused and involved in a favorite pursuit, when we are so absorbed that time flies. *El duende,* our own inner genie, yearns to be released and expressed. I believe Anne Morrow Lindbergh was referring to *el duende* when she said, "If you let yourself be absorbed completely, if you surrender completely to the moments as they pass, you live more richly those moments."

The purpose of hobbies is to become absorbed, to have fun, and to put a twinkle in your eye. You don't have to do these things well. You do them merely to experience joy. Pleasurable hobbies or even one-shot activities that you've been longing to try are an antidote for stress, a recipe for fun, and let you commune with your soul. They leave you glowing and joyful.

> Pleasurable hobbies or even one-shot activities that you've been longing to try are an antidote for stress, a recipe for fun, and let you commune with your soul.

What hobbies allow *el duende* to emerge for you? Which of your favorite pursuits have fallen by the wayside? What pleasurable activities have you always wanted to try? What interests, amusements or diversions bring you pleasure? What are you passionate about? Remember all work and no play leaves you exhausted at the end of the day. Get back in touch with *el duende* and make your soul sing!

25. What's New?

"The great source of pleasure is variety."

-Samuel Johnson

Stuck in a rut? Tired of your life? Of yourself? Just plain bored? Remember in your youth when everything seemed brand-new and you experienced life like a kid with your nose pressed against the window of a candy store? Children are engaged in a constant search for things that bring them joy and pleasure. We have repeatedly heard the old cliché; "Variety is the spice of life." How much spice have you been adding to your life lately?

Varied activities and pursuits are fun energy boosters. Variety is the spice that stimulates curiosity and challenges us intellectually. Yet it is easy to become encrusted in routine. Life becomes dull and boring when we don't have to think, when we merely act out of routine. We all thrive on diversions and variety. Variety is exhilarating!

Adding spice to your life may require some planning and thought. Why not start clipping articles out of magazines and newspapers about new and/or different restaurants to visit, upcoming events, or attractions that you've never explored? Explore some place in your own town that you've never visited. Ask friends about new things and places they've discovered and enjoyed. **Caution:** Do *not* wait until you have the time to try out these activities to begin thinking about what you'd like to do, because you may be too tired to be creative. Instead, create an ongoing "fun file" from which you can pull ideas whenever you are ready for play and adventure.

Perhaps there is a movie you've always wanted to see but haven't gotten around to renting. Or a recipe you've always wanted to try that you haven't yet prepared. (Bart found that example amusing since he tells people we store sweaters in our oven.) Anything that is new, novel, and stimulating *for you* could add that spice you crave and increase your fun quotient.

I like to think of these *spicy* activities as adult adventures. Remember the make believe adventures you and your friends created as children? Remember all of the places you explored through these adventures? That's the excitement you'll want to capture. Mae West summed up this need for variety beautifully when she said, "Whenever I have to choose between two evils, I always choose the one I haven't tried before."

> **What could you do to increase your fun quotient?**

Adults crave variety. For some, travel provides variety and adventure. I have a restless appetite for adventure and I love to travel, but it's not always financially possible, or time prohibits a get away. Perhaps you run into similar constraints. So what are some *other ways* you can add that spice and adventure to your life? Why not check out a book about France or Tahiti for a short escape? Rent a Cozumel travel video and make a Mexican dinner to create a stimulating experience. (If you go to Cozumel, the Conga line at *Carlos and Charlie's* is definitely an adventure!) Nourish your imagination! Play with ideas for bringing a sense of fun, variety, and adventure into your life.

One of my fellow career counselors wears a button that

says, "Life is *not* a dress rehearsal." Don't miss out on all life has to offer. Life is full of possibilities. Become a life explorer. It's time to add some pizzazz to your life and escape the ordinary. Be unpredictable. Go kick up your heels! Spice up your life!

What steps will you take to create an exciting exploit? What would make you feel unreservedly happy and adventurous? How can you add fun and spice to your life TODAY? Create a life full of exploration, surprises and delirious pleasures. How will you respond the next time you are asked, "What's new?"

> Become a life explorer. It's time to add some pizzazz to your life and escape the ordinary.

26. Who Do You Play With?

"A friend may well be reckoned a masterpiece of nature."

-Ralph Waldo Emerson

Who's your best friend? Who do you share your most intimate secrets with? As a teenager, I remember lying on my bed for *hours* and pouring out my hopes, my dreams, my deepest feelings, thoughts, and fears to my best friend, Angie, over that marvelous invention the telephone. Of course, I had my own phone line into the house—a survival tactic that my clever parents devised to enable other family members to receive calls between 1971 and 1973.

Angie and I were in the same sorority, Pep Club, you name it and we were in it TOGETHER. We frequently double dated—football players, naturally. Angie always understood me. We shared clothes, fashion tips, makeup, and a passion for chocolate. Our friendship outlasted many of our relationships with boys. Only college, at opposite ends of the elongated state of Virginia, and the tremendous growth that college brought each of us, caused our friendship to fade.

It is natural for friendships to ebb and flow due to life

transitions. I still feel close to Angie when I see her at class reunions. We share treasured memories, and a sense of personal history. Angie serves as an anchor to my past, a witness to my youth.

Developing friendships is a process that occurs throughout our lifetimes. What do you look for in current friendships? Are you selective when choosing friends? Do you surround yourself with people who make you feel good about yourself? Take a moment and evaluate your relationships.

One essential characteristic of healthy friendships is a *balance* between giving and receiving. Healthy friendships are reciprocal. Are you and your friends able to exchange small favors? Personal and professional guidance?

My friend Susan serves as a personal and professional guide for me. Susan is my coach. I can always count on her to give me honest, yet tactful input. She helps me grow. Susan listens and helps me formulate my goals, helps me seek out appropriate resources, and then follows up to help me take the necessary action to reach those goals. Susan stimulates me intellectually, and is one of my greatest supporters. I give to Susan in the same ways and believe that we derive a *mutual benefit* from our relationship. We are both enriched and more effective because of our friendship.

> Robert Louis Stevenson wrote, "A friend is a present you give yourself." Give yourself a present and call a playmate.

Other friends tend to stimulate and nurture our playful side. My friends Lin and June are friends that I *play* with. They enliven my life. We enjoy being together, and getting wild and wacky. We've shopped and explored New York City together (I cherish pictures we took while trying on outrageous hats in Saks), gone to comedy clubs, tried out new restaurants, etc. We can always count on lots of laughter when we are together, and that laughter is energizing.

It's important to select nurturing, positive friends. Avoid people who continually point out your faults, or those that experience a long stream of *self-created* problems. Such individuals bring you down too. They are psychological vampires who can suck the life and energy right out of you.

What's the quality of each of your friendships? Are your friends nurturing and supportive? Do you have friends to play with? Friends that stimulate you intellectually, encourage you to take risks, and help you grow? Which friends make you laugh, feel supported, and value yourself? Who helps you enjoy and appreciate life? Who would you like to add to your circle of friends? The synergy of a new friendship can enrich both of your lives.

Do you make time to be with your friends? I find time with my friends to be rejuvenating. Robert Louis Stevenson wrote, "A friend is a present you give yourself." Give yourself a present and call a playmate.

27 • A Treasure Trove of Fun

> "The world is your playground.
> Why aren't you playing?"
>
> -Ellie Katz

When I left home my very practical father made sure that I had a tool chest stocked with a hammer, screwdrivers, pliers, nails, and an assortment of other goodies for emergencies. Maybe you were given a similar array of tools to help you be prepared to take care of yourself.

> "Work at play, play at work."

My toolbox has come in handy throughout the years and I have added to it. Wonder why we aren't encouraged to build and add to our *toy* chests as we leave home? Why not build a treasure trove of fun?

I decided I needed to remedy this lack in my life and have been collecting toys that make me smile. I use these toys both at home and at work. My motto is "Work at play, play at work."

Toys are the *tools* of childhood, and when brought forward into adulthood, they help us remain playful, tap into our creativity and cope with stress. My toy box contains foam stress balls that help me release tension by either squeezing them or throwing them up against a wall depending on current stress levels. My toy box also contains lighthearted items such as a bike horn that makes a funny "honk," and a toy sword that expands to become longer and longer as it is drawn from its scabbard to help me wrestle with any dragons that cross my path. My kaleidoscope reminds me to get a new perspective or to approach a problem from a new direction.

> **Why not work happier, instead of harder?**

Gene Perret said, "A spirit of fun should pervade every meeting because it helps people participate and learn." Are your meetings as much fun as you would like? Do others look forward to attending them? One sales manager that I worked with gave a rubber chicken to the sales team member with the lowest monthly numbers. Each month they had a special ceremony to pass the chicken on to someone else. The chicken served as a playful motivator. Nobody wanted it two months in a row.

People in my workshops laugh when I use props. They often ask me to honk the horn again, and some participants come up and play with the toys during breaks. I like to use Freddie the Frog when making certain points about effective communication skills. Months after a presentation, I received letters about Freddie and how this visual tool has helped work groups to *remember my points* and significantly improve their communication skills.

Infuse your life with the spirit of fun! The spirit of fun and its partner, laughter, will help you achieve mental clarity and meet challenges creatively on even the most stressful days. In *The Artist's Way* Julia Cameron notes, "A little fun can go a long way toward making your work feel more like play" (p.19). Why not work happier, instead of harder?

Do you have a toy chest? A special container filled with playful goodies for presentations, stressful moments or to perk up a rainy day? Might your customers, clients, or coworkers remember points that you make *longer* if you inserted a bit of levity into their days? Try it. Visit a toy store and engage in a bit of whimsy.

The great thing about being an adult is you can buy your own toys. Was there some toy you *always* wanted as a child but never received? Now is your chance. Go out and get that special treasure. Add a bit of pizzazz to your day. Toys put gladness in your soul and joy in your heart. What have you got to lose? Work at play, play at work

> **Infuse your life with the spirit of fun! The spirit of fun and its partner, laughter, will help you achieve mental clarity and meet challenges creatively on even the most stressful days.**

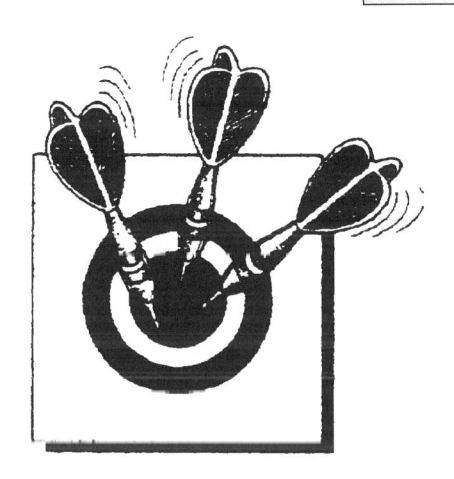

28 • Absent or Present?

"Life becomes so much simpler when we take time to enjoy the simple pleasures of nature."

-Marjolein Bastin

Children focus on enjoyment RIGHT NOW. They live in the present with a sense of joyfulness and play. Children seek to experience each moment to the fullest. They live in the *present*, not in the future or the past.

I love watching my six-month-old granddaughter, McKenzie. She is *totally* involved in the present. When playing with a toy, McKenzie has a laser-like focus and is not easily distracted. Her body, mind, and soul are committed to her current endeavor.

Are you living in the present and noticing the beauty and the simple pleasures that surround you every day?

Living in and enjoying the present moment is one of the best-kept secrets for stress reduction and wellness, in addition to adding to your daily fun quotient. As we hurry through life with our minds racing ahead to all of the things

> Living in and enjoying the present moment is one of the best-kept secrets for stress reduction and wellness, in addition to adding to your daily fun quotient.

we need to do, we frequently miss the opportunity to enjoy life's abundant pleasures.

Do you focus on the present? Are you attuned to the awesome details of nature? Are you taking time to enjoy each singular moment? These are *rejuvenating* childhood qualities that many adults replace with the *hurry up syndrome*, choosing to hurtle through life at the speed of light *instead* of savoring the uniqueness of each moment and nature's simple pleasures. Natural pleasures make up our *immediate surroundings* every day. They are gifts for our enjoyment; gifts to savor.

Last night I took pleasure in noticing how very beautiful the sunset was. At first the darkening sky was painted with lovely yellow, salmon, and pink brush strokes which became richer and deepened into red licks of fire. Varying degrees of orange and finally purple soon joined the wildly colorful, flickering pageant. It was as if I had my very own fireworks show, brightly glimmering and vibrant. I truly enjoy sunsets, and *used* to only take time to notice them when we were vacationing on some relaxing Caribbean Island. Sunsets in Richmond, Virginia are moments to be treasured and enjoyed as well!

Other simple pleasures available to all of us include noticing the ducks and geese that are drawn to nearby lakes. We are fortunate to have a toaster-testing center for a national appliance maker on a lake right up the street from us. The center is a popular place at lunchtime because some of the workers feed our feathered friends toast.

The birds are smart and there is usually a flock of them waiting patiently for their treats near the testing center door. I'm glad they toss out *toast*, because, as Bart explained, "If they toasted bagels I would be out there lined up with the ducks."

Don't let life pass you by! How can you spend more time enjoying the present moment? How can you savor the uniqueness of today? List ten simple pleasures that you can easily enjoy.

Select one of these ten simple pleasures and invest five to ten minutes in enjoying the present moment. It's *now* that matters. Abandon all other thoughts and just enjoy this simple pleasure.

What benefit did you derive from focusing on the present moment? Would the quality of your life be different if you took ten minutes every week to focus on the present moment? Every day? Over time the quality of your life will improve dramatically if you forego *absenteeism* and consciously choose to be present.

29. Does a Puppeteer Pull Your Strings?

"Guilt is the gift that keeps on giving."

-Anonymous

Puppet shows have always been a source of great fascination to me. I admire the puppeteer's creativity, his or her ability to entertain others, to weave a captivating story and to get viewers caught up in the plot of the story. It entrances me to watch children become so engrossed in the story that they talk back to the puppets as if they were real.

We all carry with us an internal puppeteer that has an enormous impact on our moods, our self-confidence, our self-esteem, and our ability to take action. Our internal puppeteer carries on a silent conversation that only we can hear. It whispers to us almost continually, and much of what it says keeps us from experiencing fun and causes us to feel guilt.

Guilt is a form of internal stress that can interfere with our ability to enjoy life, to relax, and to play. We all experience guilt. We are taught to feel guilty at a young age by family members, teachers, through messages we receive from the church, and later by the media and all of those commercials/ads which knaw away at our insecurities.

The puppeteer's words tend to echo those early messages that we received from significant others in our lives, and focus on guilt producers such as have to, must, should, ought to, and got to. In addition to making us feel guilty, these words are judgmental, and make us feel like victims who have *no choice* regarding our actions. Instead of making a *conscious choice*, we get into the habit of letting the puppeteer pulls our strings, and we *automatically* jump.

> Give your puppeteer some time off!! Send it on a long vacation, and from now on let your playful inner funster pull the strings for a more pleasant, enjoyable life.

Your internal puppeteer tends to drive you mercilessly to do *more* even when you are tired. Although you have already put in a full day, it nags you with messages like, "You *have to* clean the house. You *ought to* change the beds. You *must* wash and dry clothes. You *should* bake goods for your family instead of buying them," etc., etc. Perfection in all things is the puppeteer's ideal, and if its should-ought-must voice is strong, it swats you every time you fall short of that ideal.

Your internal puppeteer also operates from the old childhood rule that "You have to get all of your work done *before* you can play." WRONG! This outmoded rule is no longer applicable to us now that we are grown-ups with a never-ending range of obligations and responsibilities.

Want to feel like a kid again? Want more fun in your life? Don't *should* on yourself! Begin to reprogram your inner puppeteer. Instead of being *ordered* around by guilt producing words, select words of *choice* such as "I want to," "I prefer to," "I choose to," or "It would be to my advantage to." These words of choice are both non-judgmental and motivational. They imply that you have a choice and that choice can be to have fun!

The next time your inner puppeteer starts trying to manipulate you into doing something that you don't feel like doing, cut the strings! From now on listen to your playful, inner fun-ster. What does he/she need? Perhaps your inner fun-ster would prefer to play a game, to go to a movie, or to prop your feet up and call a friend for a giggle or two. Give your puppeteer the day off! Send it on a long vacation, and let your playful inner fun-ster pull the strings for a more pleasant, enjoyable life.

30 · Go Dilly-Dally!

"It's not enough to be busy; so are ants.
The question is: What are we busy about?"

-Henry David Thoreau

I believe the reason that I still love to learn today is because I was fortunate to have very loving, nurturing and accepting teachers UNTIL…Dah! Dah! Dah! DAHHHHH!…I reached the fifth grade and things changed. My next experience was with a matron who must have student taught in the Nazi Germany. She was unsmiling, harsh, rule-driven, and nothing we did was ever good enough.

Do you remember the section on your report card that said, "Uses time wisely"? Well of course, "Always" was not checked on my report card that year. I remember being told not to dilly-dally and look out of the window after I finished all of my work. "Find something else to do. Be productive!" was Brun Hilda's cry.

Her intention, I am certain, was to instill in us a strong sense of personal responsibility and a highly defined work ethic. Yet, even today, when I think of her I still hear the Wicked Witch of the West's theme song from the *Wizard of Oz* in my head.

A strong work ethic is a hard concept for impulsive, pleasure-seeking children to buy in to, but after consistent reinforcement over decades, we internalize the message. Especially youngsters who are motivated by rewards like good grades, gold stars, and compliments.

Some of us learn too well, and as adults have an *overdeveloped* sense of duty and obligation; a compulsion to *do*. We constantly strive to meet all of our personal and professional responsibilities to the best of our abilities. We mercilessly drive ourselves to work hard, often reaching multiple goals simultaneously, and to focus on the *products* we are producing, yet long for time to enjoy the *process* of living—time to dilly-dally.

After being programmed to focus on producing *products* for so many years, we tend to forget that we can choose anything else, and much needed fun and relaxation becomes virtually impossible. The choice to notice and enjoy the beauty of a spring day, to daydream, or to hang out and do nothing becomes foreign to our worlds.

This brings us back to Thoreau's question, "What are we busy about?" Is it to avoid feeling lazy? I find comfort short periods of laziness and dilly-dallying. These periods serve to refresh and recharge my weary mind, body, and spirit. I emerge from a short lazy period with renewed energy to tackle difficult

> While visiting Don Quixote's La Mancha, I heard an old Spanish proverb that I have typed up and strategically placed in a number of spots where I will see it often. It reads "How beautiful it is to do nothing, and then to rest afterward." What a revolutionary thought; one to savor.

tasks, and quite often, with new creative ways to solve problems, even though I was not consciously aware that I was working to solve them. As Cicero noted, "Only the person who is relaxed can create, and to that mind ideas flow like lightning."

While visiting Don Quixote's La Mancha this spring, I heard an old Spanish proverb that I have typed up and strategically placed in a number of spots where I will see it often. It reads, "How beautiful it is to do nothing, and then to rest afterward." What a revolutionary thought; one to savor. Sounds like a worthwhile quest to me!

Now that we are no longer receiving grades regarding "Uses time wisely," how long has it been since *you* did nothing? Since you dawdled? Do you ever stare out into space to give your mind and body the opportunity to rest and recharge for a few lovely, luxurious, lazy moments? Doing nothing reduces stress levels, builds energy and boosts creativity. Wouldn't you say that's a worthy investment of time? An investment with valuable dividends? Get busy . . . doing absolutely nothing! **Go dilly-dally!**

Bibliography

Ackerman, D. *A Natural History of the Senses.* New York: Random House, 1990.

Bedrosian, M. M. *Life is More Than Your To-Do List: Blending Business Success with Personal Satisfaction.* Rockville, MD: BCI Press, 1995.

Cameron, J. *The Artist's Way: A Spiritual Path to Higher Creativity.* New York: G. P. Putnam's Sons, 1992.

Chillot, R. "Don't Shun the Sun", *Prevention,* March 1998, Volume 50, Issue 3, p.27.

Dyer, W. W. *The Secrets to Manifesting Your Destiny (audiocassette program).* Niles, IL: Nightingale-Conant, Corp., 1994.

Eyre, L. and R. *Lifebalance: How to Simplify and Bring Harmony to Your Everyday Life.* New York: Fireside, 1997.

Goad, K. *Magic Moments: A Busy Woman's Guide to Forgotten Pleasures.* Salt Lake City, UT: Commune-a-Key Publishing, 1997.

Godek, G. J. P. *1001 Ways to be Romantic.* Boston: Casablanca Press, Inc., 1993.

Gregory, M. *Stress-Free in 15 Minutes (audiotape/CD).* Richmond, VA: Living Successfully, Inc., 1998.

Gregory, M. *Up With Energy, Down With Stress! (audiotape).* Richmond, VA: Living Successfully, Inc., 2000.

Hightower, K. *Simple Joys: Little Things That Make a BIG Difference.* Alexandria, VA: Quick Study Press, 1998.

Howerton, G. *Hit Any Key to Energize: A Caffeine-Free Guide to Perk Up Your Spirits.* Alexandria, VA: Quick Study Press, 1997.

LaRoche, L. *Relax - You May Only Have a Few Minutes Left: Using the Power of Humor to Overcome Stress in Your Life and Work.* New York: Villard Books, 1998.

Lawless, J. *The Complete Guide to Aromatherapy: A Practical Approach to the Use of Essential Oils for Health and Well-being.* Boston: Element Books Limited, 1997.

Leider, R. J. *Life Skills: Taking Charge of Your Personal and Professional Growth.* San Diego: Pfeiffer & Company, 1994.

Lindberg, A. W. *Gift From the Sea.* New York: Pantheon Books, 1975.

Maas, J. B. *Power Sleep: The Revolutionary Program That Prepares Your Mind for Peak Performance.* New York: Random House, 1998.

McLaughlin, P. *Catch Fire: A 7-Step Program to Ignite Energy, Defuse Stress, and Power Boost Your Career.* New York: Fawcett Columbine, 1998.

Metcalfe, C. W. and R. Felible. *Lighten Up: Survival Skills for People Under Pressure.* Reading, MA: Addison-Wesley Publishing Company, Inc., 1992.

Sanford, L. T. and M. E. Donovan. *Women and Self-Esteem: Understanding and Improving the Way We Think and Feel About Ourselves.* New York: Penguin Books, 1984.

Thayer, R. E. *The Origin of Everyday Moods: Managing Energy, Tension, and Stress.* New York: Oxford University Press, 1996.

Wilson, P. *Instant Calm: Over 100 Easy-to-Use Techniques for Relaxing Mind and Body.* New York: Dutton Signet, 1995.

Helpful Organization

The Humor Project, Inc. 110 Spring Street, Saratoga Springs, NY 12866. Dr. Joel Goodman. 1(518) 587-8770.

Focuses on the positive power of humor and creativity. Provides programs and resources to improve the effectiveness and quality of life for individuals and organizations. The Humor Project Catalog is loaded with books, videos, audiotapes, games, computer software, props, and their "Laughing Matters" magazine. They also hold an annual humor and creativity conference.

Practical Tools to Revitalize Your Life

Keynote speaker/trainer

Dr. Mitzi Gregory offers speaking and training sessions to help organizations energize and motivate employees, enhance team productivity, and effectively manage stress. Mitzi has delivered upbeat presentations and interactive workshops to a wide range of audiences including numerous professional associations, manufacturing, government, finance, higher education, and health care.

The next time you want to rejuvenate your employees, renew your commitment to work/life balance, or relax after a particularly stressful time, let Dr. Mitzi revitalize your group with a customized presentation or onsite training.

- Up With Energy, Down With Stress
- Overworked and Underplayed? Quick, Easy Ways to Enhance Productivity and Boost Motivation
- Enhancing Team Effectiveness
- Career Coaching for Managers
- Managing Stress With Finesse

Other Revitalizing Tools

STRESS-FREE IN 15 MINUTES©

—De-stress with this relaxing audio program $10.00

UP WITH ENERGY, DOWN WITH STRESS!©
—Audiotape recorded live $10.00

Visit Mitzi online at *www.DrMitzi.com* to order these and other practical tools or send a check or money order to:

Gregory Training Associates, Inc.

4631 Four Seasons Terrace, Suite F, Glen Allen, VA 23060
804.273.0304 Phone • 804.273.1945 Fax
DrMGregory@aol.com